12 SIMPLE SECRETS

^{TO} FINDING
FULFILLMENT
at work

12 SIMPLE SECRETS

ᵀᴼ FINDING FULFILLMENT
at work

Orlando, Florida

12 Simple Secrets to Finding Fulfillment at Work
by Glenn Van Ekeren

Published by HigherLife Development Services, Inc.
242 Westminster Terrace
Oviedo, Florida 32765
(407) 563-4806
www.ahigherlife.com

Cover Design: DaNita Naimoli

ISBN 13: 978-0-9793227-8-5
ISBN 10: 0-9793227-8-2

09 10 11 12 13 — 8 7 6 5 4 3 2 1

Printed in the United States of America

Contents

Introduction 1

Section One—
Passion: Infuse Your Work With Passion

1. Light Yourself on Fire 4
2. The Money Is the Gravy 7
3. Contentment Breeds Discontentment 10
4. There's No Need To Be Miserable 13

Section Two—
Learning: Good Enough Never Is

5. Learners Will Inherit the Future 18
6. Grow Beyond Where You Are..................................21
7. Prepare for the Future 23
8. Settling for Nothing Less Than Wow!..................26

Section Three—
Ownership: Become the Own in Ownership

9.   Act Like an Owner 30

10. Take the Time To Fix Your Leaky Boat 33

11. Don't Hold Back 38

12. Making a Difference 40

Section Four—
Investment: Give Your Best to What Matters Most

13. Take a Few Minutes To Think About Time 44

14. Learn To Schedule Your Priorities 49

15. I Know You're Busy, But What Are You Getting Done? ... 52

16. Take Your Job and Love It! 55

Section Five—
Ability: Tap Into Your Talent

17. Focus On What You Do Best 60

18. Achievement Has No Finish Line 63

19. Dig a Little Deeper 67

20. Rethink What You Think 72

Section Six—
Attitude: The Anchor of Attitude

21. Make Every Hour a Happy Hour 76

22. Do What You Love and Success Will Follow 79

23. Career-Building Principles 81

24. Know What You Value and Live It............................. 89

Section Seven—
Improvement: Build a Better You

25.	Pay Attention to Who You Are	94
26.	Getting a Better View of Yourself	97
27.	Be the Best You Can Be	101
28.	Jump in … You'll Get Used to It	105

Section Eight—
Action: Make Things Happen

29.	Complete Uncompleted Tasks	108
30.	Half Finished	111
31.	Filling Holes or Planting Trees	113
32.	There Are Only So Many Tomorrows	115

Section Nine—
Development: Success Is Where You Find It

33.	Developing Your Picture of Success	120
34.	What Impression Would You Have Made?	124
35.	The Makings of Success	129
36.	Face Your Challenges Head On	131

Section Ten—
Risks: Break New Ground

37.	It's Not That Bad!	136
38.	Move Through Your Fears	140
39.	Spring Back to Life	143
40.	Live Like There's No Tomorrow	146

Section Eleven—
Cooperation: Be a Team Player

41.   Become a Trust Builder 150

42.   We Are the Team 154

43.   Practice the Art of Encouragement 158

44.   Acquiring an Awesome Attitude.......................... 161

Section Twelve—
Joyfulness: Lo0sen Up…Lighten Up…Have Fun!

45.   An Entertaining Flight Attendant........................168

46.   Put Your Work in Perspective 170

47.   Refills Are Free 173

48.   Have a Little Fun...175

Endnotes...177

ACKNOWLEDGMENTS

I'M CONTINUALLY GRATEFUL TO MY parents who taught me the value of work at an early age, provided the example of a good work ethic, and encouraged me to give my best at whatever I did.

Thank you to my wife, Marty, and my children, Matt and Katy, for helping me to keep my work in perspective. You are the joy of my life.

INTRODUCTION

I'VE WORKED A VARIETY OF jobs in my lifetime. As I made my way through high school and college, I did everything from laying sod balls to lugging steel to being an ecology specialist (garbage hauler) to washing dishes in the college cafeteria to working as a camp counselor, which allowed me to sleep in a tent for ten weeks one summer. These less-than-glamorous jobs involved a lot of mundane tasks and got downright boring at times. I often marveled at the work I was willing to do just to make some money when the paycheck seemed like a minor reward.

Most of us have endured such work experiences and learned at an early age that every job seemed to require doing a lot of things we didn't like to do. Daydreaming often became my escape from those small, dull, routine jobs. Although I loved to dream about achieving some exciting career, my real-world experiences got me to thinking that any career I chose in the future would probably require me to perform less-than-desired tasks. And I was right.

The challenge was to concentrate and focus my energies on the things I liked to do. This simple discovery transformed the way I approach work and paved the way for experiencing many years of work fulfillment and career satisfaction. IBM executive Buck Rogers once said, "Our work has to be more than an unfortunate necessity, an unpleasant means of paying the bills. We owe it to ourselves and to the people who are important to us to demand more out of all those hours. It's our responsibility to make sure our work gives us the pleasure of pride, accomplishment, and congenial relationships."[1]

People who expect their work to totally fulfill them, their salary to always be what they want it to be, and their careers to continue including only things they enjoy doing are going to be gravely disappointed. It is our responsibility to make our career more than just a means to making a living. Your job can be wonderful or miserable. The difference depends on you.

12 Simples Secrets to Finding Fulfillment at Work takes a refreshing look at what work can be. It rethinks our approach to work. As we struggle in today's pursuit of jobs in a struggling economy, these stories can have a major influence in each of our vocational situations.

Whatever your chosen career, get into it. Stop looking at work as simply a means of making a living or the price you pay to climb a corporate ladder. Understand that work is an essential ingredient in making a quality life. When you drench yourself in what you do, the rewards will follow.

Section One

Passion: Infuse Your Work With Passion

Chapter 1

LIGHT YOURSELF ON FIRE

Motivation is a fire from within. If someone else tries to light that fire under you, chances are it will burn briefly.

Stephen Covey[1]

O NCE UPON A TIME THERE was a guy named Joe who had a very lousy job." Those are the opening words of Stephen Speilberg's 1990 movie, *Joe Versus The Volcano.*[2]

In the movie, Joe Banks (Tom Hanks) reaches a point of total frustration with his job and his life. Every day is a bad Monday. His boss is always in a bad mood. The cumulative stresses convince Joe his energy-stripped life is irreparable. Exasperated and depressed, he laments, "I'm losing my soul." Soon after Joe learns he is plagued with terminal "brain cloud" (a fictitious diagnosis that convinced Joe he was mentally asleep).

Unemployed and desperate, Joe coincidentally encounters an eccentric jillionaire (played by Lloyd Bridges) who presents a proposition that allows Joe to turn his mediocre, dead-end, unfulfilled life around. All he must do in return is journey to the island of Waponi Woo and leap into a volcano. Joe leaps at the chance.

Aboard the jillionaire's yacht, Joe meets Patricia, one of the wealthy man's daughters. In awe of the incredible turn of events and the new life he has enjoyed since meeting her father, Joe looks into the moonless, star-filled night and exclaims, "Your life is unbelievable—just unbelievable!"

Patricia's response was profound. "My father says that almost the whole world is asleep—everybody you know, everybody you see, everybody you talk to. He says that only a few people are awake, and they live in a state of constant, total amazement."

The movie was a commercial disaster and a popular target of cynical movie critics who missed this scene, or at least misinterpreted the writer's attempt at jolting people into "waking up."

Paul Goodman, the famous linguist and social commentator, estimated that as many as 82 percent of American workers don't like being at work and can't wait to be freed from what work does to them.[3] They are the "Joe Banks" of the world who need an immediate wake-up call, preferably (for them) without the threat of terminal "brain cloud."

People who depend on others for the condition of their morale do themselves a huge disservice. No organization or supervisor can adequately be empowered to pump you up.

It's so popular today to plead victimization by the system, circumstances, competition, rightsizing or other external factors. Human spirits are buffeted by increased pressures from co-workers, job demands, or the daily grind of everyday living. Indifference slithers in to replace motivation, and a vicious cycle of unhappiness begins.

Blaming, finger-pointing, and accusing are popular anecdotes for attitudes gone sour. Steer free from such self-defeating behavior. Take charge of your moods. Fill your energy tank. Corral negative emotions. Bury grudges and perceived unfairness. Recognize your present mental attitudes about the job and get serious about an action plan to help you out of the ruts.

Are you alive with excitement about your work? Are you doing what you love? Light yourself on fire. Become a passionate, self-igniting morale arsonist rather than operating on the erroneous assumption that someone else will make your job more exciting or more challenging.

I often ask applicants what prompted them to apply to our organization. It never ceases to amaze me how many people respond, "I thought you might have a job I would like." Sorry. We don't have any jobs like that. However, we do have a lot of people who like their jobs.

Your job (no matter how great or lousy it is) can be more than a way to earn a living. Make it an important element in creating a quality life. You don't need to jump into a volcano to light yourself on fire. Reenergizing your work spirit is an inside job.

> Success is not the result of spontaneous combustion. You must set yourself on fire.
>
> Reggie Leach[4]

Chapter 2

THE MONEY IS THE GRAVY

To fulfill a dream, to be allowed to sweat over lonely labor, to be given a chance to create, is the meat and potatoes of life. The money is the gravy.

Bette Davis[1]

DENIS WAITLEY, IN *Empires of the Mind,* shared the experience of attending his daughter's college graduation. Fearing the exercises would be long and merciless, Waitley was relieved when the keynote speaker took the podium. The speaker was Edward James Olmos, the actor-activist who played Jaime Excalante in *Stand and Deliver,* an inspiring movie about inner-city students.

Olmos stood up, removed his cap, and regarded the graduates. "So we're ready to party?" he asked. "Yeah, let's party!" they answered in unison. "I know, thank God it's Friday," he resumed, "But commencement means to begin, not finish. You've had a four-year sabbatical from life, and now you're ready to go out there and earn. You're only beginning Real World 101 in your education."

"One more thing before we leave," he continued. "Please never, ever work for money. Please don't just get a job. A job is something that many of you had while you were working your way through college. A job is something you do for money. But a career is something you do because you must do it. You want to do it, you love doing it, you're excited when you do it. And you'd do it even if you were paid nothing beyond food and basics. You do it because it's your life."[2]

Rarely does our educational training prepare us to find a career that is satisfying. We go to college, learn skills and then find a company that offers a paycheck in exchange for our knowledge and a few hours of work. If only we could inject every college graduate and potential employee with this admonishment, "Pursue a passion, not a paycheck." This simple insight could save a multitude of people from being disillusioned. Charles Schwab, steel magnate, concluded: "The man who does not work for the love of work but only for money is not likely to make money nor find much fun in life."[3] No matter how little or how much your chosen career pays in money, if you pursue it with passion, you'll go to work every day with the satisfaction of knowing you are making a difference.

We all need the money. That is a given. But, work goes beyond what you do to earn a paycheck; it involves personal commitment, personal satisfaction, and personal growth. Like it or not, these results along with promotions and pay increases are rewards for achieving results, not just doing work. Results are realized when we apply and develop our strengths. In *Good By Job, Hello Me*, Wexler and Wolf suggest, "The fascination of simply making money wears thin in time. The real fruits of one's labors are seen in the planting of one's gifts."[4] When you are involved in a company that shares your values and you are doing a job that utilizes your talents and skills, a meaningful career will blossom.

"Is my occupation what I get paid money for, or is it something larger and wider and richer— more a matter of what I am or how I think about myself," questioned Robert Fulghum. "Making a living and having a life are not the same thing. Making a living and making a life that's worthwhile are not the same thing. A job title doesn't even come close to answering the question, 'What do you do?' Possessing a title or allowing money to possess you does not answer the questions, 'Who are you?' or 'What do you do?'"[5]

How many people do you know working in a job they dislike so they can earn enough money to do the things they like to do? What a dead-end, dissatisfying, unfulfilling way to approach a job.

Historically, people have viewed work as a required necessity to make a living, but actually living was reserved for after hours. Times are changing. There's a visible epidemic among people questioning what they really want out of life and work. A paycheck and a few benefits are no longer sufficient to generate passion and achieve meaning. People want jobs that matter. Tom Brokaw said, "It's easy to make a buck. It's a lot tougher to make a difference."[6] What makes this difficult is discovering for ourselves what activities are meaningful and allow us the opportunity to make a difference. If you've been feeling disenfranchised, unmotivated, dissatisfied, or apathetic, there's a chance you've not yet realized that it takes more than money to light the fire of passion.

Immerse yourself in whatever you are doing. Don't go to work because you have to. Go to work to make a difference. Instead of complaining that you can't find a job you like, concentrate on what you like about your job. Transform your thinking and design strategies to creatively enhance the contribution you make. View yourself as a little company inside of the larger one. Hold yourself accountable for the success of your department. You are the organization. What you do matters. And remember, "The money is the gravy."

> First find something you like to do so much you'd gladly do it for nothing; then learn to do it so well people are happy to pay you for it.
>
> Walt Disney[7]

Chapter 3

CONTENTMENT BREEDS DISCONTENTMENT

If I see myself today as I was in the past, my past must resurrect itself and become my future.

William James[1]

I T'S DANGEROUS TO REST ON our past successes. In the book, *The Eighty-Yard Run,* a college freshman at his first football practice, breaks loose for an eighty-yard touchdown run. His teammates immediately place him in high esteem and the coach lets him know he will have quite a future with the team. His pretty blond girlfriend picks him up after practice and awards him with a passionate kiss. He has the feeling his life is now set, his future secure.

Unfortunately, nothing in his life ever matches that day again. His football experiences never rise above the level of mediocrity, nor does his business career. His marriage goes sour and the disappointment is even greater because he continually reflects back on that day of glory when he was convinced that life would always be pleasant and act favorably toward him.[2]

This young man, and the rest of humankind for that matter, could learn something from Wisconsin dairy industry. On the side of their milk bottles are printed these words: "Our cows are not contented. They're anxious to do better."[3]

Contentment breeds discontentment. When you're satisfied with savoring the past in lieu of creating your future, the present loses its appeal. Aspiring to excel, our last achievement inspires us to grow beyond the present. Continuing to think about the same things day after day or attempting to build our lives based on the past is anti-productive. Don't get me wrong, your past is important, but only to the degree your experiences inspire you to new levels of living. Life is more meaningful when you are searching for ways to exceed your past performance, not be content with it.

There is a *Peanuts* cartoon in which Charlie Brown says to Linus: "For as long as I've lived, whenever I put on my shoes, I've always put the left one on first…then suddenly, last week I put the right one on first. Every day this week I've been putting my right shoe on first, and you know what? It hasn't changed my life a bit."[4] New levels are not precipitated by changing which shoe you put on first. I'm talking here about more essential choices. There is more of a price to pay. I am well aware of the tendency for people to quit growing, risking and moving forward when the price gets too high.

Johann Wolfgang von Goethe hit a nerve when he said, "Things that matter most must never be at the mercy of things that matter least."[5] Contentment with your favorite foods, road to work, most watched television programs, and most frequently worn outfit is fine—although I would suggest a little variation to put some spice in your life. These are trivial issues compared to the performance practices, habits, attitudes, approach to problems, relationship skills and other "most" items Goethe alluded to, that significantly impact your future success.

Fight hard to remain free of long term contentment and satisfaction with your former accomplishments. Strive for higher plateaus. You'll never have to look back and wish you could go there. It's exciting to work and live with positive anticipation for what can happen next. As Disney's Pocahantas said, "You'll see things you never knew you never knew."[6]

> Workers develop routines when they do the same job for a while. They lose their edge, falling into habits not just in what they do but in how they think. Habits turn into routines. Routines into ruts.
>
> Robert Kriegel[7]

Chapter 4

There's No Need to Be Miserable

When I'm happy I feel like crying, but when I'm sad I don't feel like laughing. I think it's better to be happy. Then you get two feelings for the price of one.

Lily Tomlin[1]

HOW HAPPY ARE YOU WITH your job? Are there times when misery is more prevalent than happiness?

Norman Cousins, the late author and editor of *Saturday Review*, wrote, "Happiness is probably the easiest emotion to feel, the most elusive to create deliberately, and the most difficult to define. It is experienced differently by different people."[2] Although happiness is different for each of us, here are few generic principles worth thinking about:

1. End "The Search." People who place the search for happiness as the top priority in their lives will struggle to experience it. "Happiness is a butterfly— the more you chase it, the more it flies away from you and hides," wrote Rabbi Harold Kushner in the bestselling book *When All You've Ever Wanted Isn't Enough*. "But stop chasing it, put away your net and busy yourself with other, more productive things than the pursuit of happiness, and it will sneak up on you from behind and perch on your shoulder."[3]

2. Evaluate Your Expectations. Thinking you can be happy with your job all the time is an unrealistic expectation. It won't happen, no matter how hard you try, even if you read every word in this book and implement each suggestion. When you expect your job to make you happy, you've already put yourself in a disadvantageous position. Add to this a desperate pursuit of this elusive emotion and you'll understand why so many people are miserable in their job. [5]

For the most part, I expect to enjoy a happy, satisfied, fulfilled career and when it doesn't happen, a sense of misery and discontent settles in. Within moments, I'm acutely aware of how my expectations and reality are in conflict. It's a natural set-up for disappointment. Author Max Lucado offers this valuable advice, "Remember, disappointment is caused by unmet expectations. Disappointment is cured by revamped expectations."[4] It's a huge mistake to set our expectations so high they are unattainable or depend on our work to be the sole source of happiness. The problem, of course, is that only rarely do our jobs, other people, or life in general, live up to the expected ideal.

3. Exit Your Misery. Actor and singer Dean Martin's closest friends commented upon his death that, although he had died physically, Dean Martin had given up on life years earlier. After his son died in a plane crash, Martin was vocal about his loss of interest in living. Without his son, he no longer wanted to live. Friends tried to help him through these difficult times but Martin was intent that life was over. He became a recluse, refused to see friends and spent his days watching television by himself.[6]

It's a dangerous thing to hang our happiness on the shoulders of some other person, a career, or a business. As tragic as the event was, Dean Martin still had a lot of life to live. He could have toured with his good friend Frank Sinatra, relished the offers of dinner and enjoyed fellowship with close friends, or poured himself into a number of useful causes. Instead, he gave up on life.

I certainly am not implying that our work compares in value to our relationships. Yet, when people die, life does go on. We grieve. We reflect. We cherish the good times. Expectations are adjusted. We go on. Likewise, we will experience disappointment, unmet expectations, and the death of dreams and goals in our work lives. We refocus, carefully monitoring our reactions, and push forward. It is simply a waste of time and talent to give up and give in to misery.

4. Entertain an Agenda Other Than Your Own. An article from an unknown source, "How To Be Miserable," says, "Think about yourself. Talk about yourself. Use 'I' as often as possible. Mirror yourself continually in the opinion of others. Listen greedily to what people say about you. Expect to be appreciated. Be suspicious. Be jealous and envious. Be sensitive to slights. Never forgive a criticism. Trust nobody but yourself. Insist on consideration and respect. Demand agreement with your own views on everything. Sulk if people are not grateful to you for favors shown them. Never forget a service you have rendered. Shirk your duties if you can. Do as little as possible for others."[6]

I often find the people most unhappy with their work are those who choose to constantly think about themselves and how unhappy they are. The happiest people I encounter are so busy creating and enjoying life, they don't even think about being happy. Their happiness is a by-product of the unselfish effort they put forth. Greta Palmer wisely observed, "Those only are happy who have their minds on some object other than their own happiness—on the happiness of others, on the improvement of mankind, even on some art or pursuit followed not as a means but as itself an ideal end."[7]

5. Expand Your Thinking. Dale Carnegie suggested that, "Happiness doesn't depend upon who you are or what you have; it depends solely upon what you think."[8] If you continually think about yourself—what you want, the desire for a more exciting job, dissatisfaction with your salary, the need for a vacation, a better boss or simply for the sun to shine to brighten your spirits—then misery rather than happiness will remain your companion. Remove yourself from the temptation of sponsoring a personal pity-party and do something about what you can do something about. Get on with it. You'll be amazed at how quickly your actions will modify your thinking and emotions.

6. Energize the Current Situation. Being happy in a job that isn't what you thought it would be isn't easy. If you fall into the category of the people continually dissatisfied with their jobs, there is hope. You do have a choice to be happier on the job by focusing and acting on the influences within your control. You can also decide to remain forever miserable.

Charlie "Tremendous" Jones reminds us that, "If you can't be happy where you are, it's a cinch you can't be happy where you ain't."[9] In other words, if you can't be happy now with what you have, with what you do and who you are, you will not be happy when you get what you think you want. Happiness comes with learning the skill of living each moment and making the best of it. Certain experiences, job tasks and people might make it easier for us to be happy, but they do not have the power to make you happy unless you allow them to. You have a choice to be happy or unhappy with your circumstances. Since you are one or the other, why not choose happiness?

Happiness won't resurrect itself if we sulk and brood about the fact that we aren't as happy as we think we should be or would like to be. "It's good to be just plain happy," suggests Henry Miller, "it's a little better to know that you're happy; but to understand that you're happy and to know why and how...and still be happy, be happy in the being and the knowing, well that is beyond happiness, that is bliss."[10] Master this attitude and move forward in life. Stop chasing happiness. Allow it to catch up with you.

> To experience happiness, we must train ourselves to live in this moment, to savor it for what it is, not running ahead in anticipation of some future date nor lagging behind in the paralysis of the past.
>
> Luci Swindoll[11]

Section Two

LEARNING: GOOD ENOUGH NEVER IS

Chapter 5

LEARNERS WILL INHERIT THE FUTURE

Then let us all do what is right, strive with all our might toward the unattainable, develop as fully as we can the gifts God has given us, and never stop learning.

Ludwig van Beethoven[1]

AFTER WATCHING PETER JENNINGS ON the ABC Evening News for many years, it's hard to believe that he wasn't always a smooth anchor person. His first experience, while in his twenties, did not establish him as an audience-friendly journalist.

Three years in his anchor position, Jennings made a bold move. He quit his envious position reading the news and retreated into the trenches to refine his skills as a working reporter. In their informative book, *Anchors: Brokaw, Jennings, Rather and the Evening News*, Robert Goldberg and Gerald Jay Goldberg provide an insightful look at Jenning's journey to becoming a respected TV journalist. They describe how Jennings, who never finished college, used the road as his educational classroom. He covered a wide variety of stories in the United States, became the first network correspondent on permanent assignment in the Middle East, moved to London, and covered other cities in Europe, before returning to the anchor slot at ABC.[2]

To be successful in today's business environment, one should seek hands-on experiences, intellectual stimulation, and an appreciation for information to boost effectiveness. Climbing the career ladder or attaining a positive reputation in one's current position is precipitated by the ability to learn, absorb, adapt, and apply information that keeps your skills on the cutting edge. You need to be accountable for continually auditing your skill level through self-reflection and pursuing opportunities that take your professionalism to the next level.

By reading, listening, taking risks, and gaining exposure to new experiences, you can overcome ignorance that breeds complacency and blocks career vitality. Professional competence requires a consistent updating of your skill portfolio and the ability to stimulate learning throughout your entire work life. Make your job your classroom. When your job is flowing smoothly, double your learning. When times are challenging, and the demands are high, quadruple your learning. Learning is a marvelous offense in a radically changing world.

Ironically, professional success can decelerate growth. Satisfaction with the past and present inhibits accelerated learning and adaptability. Without shifting your attitudes to a quest for expansive learning, you will lose your vitality by resting on the past. A continuum of learning ensures the removal of complacency and an increase in competency. No matter how successful you are, without investing in your personal growth, the risk of sinking into repetitious and hypnotic activity is inevitable. The key to sustained success is to keep learning. Probe, adjust, adapt, and develop in new directions.

Look for people who will challenge you. No matter how competent you are, never allow your ego to swell to the point that you shut out the expertise of others. Enlist the help of a friend, a mentor to tell you truthfully where you can grow, expand you talents or seek new possibilities. You want someone who will challenge you and inspire you to tackle the unknown. Such a friend will prove professionally invaluable.

Learn from your actions. Harvard Business School's John Kotter suggests, "You grab a challenge, act on it, then honestly reflect on why your actions worked or didn't. You learn from it and then move on. That continuous process of lifelong learning helps enormously in a rapidly changing economic environment."[3]

Learn from your experiences. If things don't work, don't keep doing them the same way and expect positive results.

Robert H. Rosen and Lisa Berger writing in *The Healthy Company* said, "To learn, an individual cannot be afraid of asking questions, making mistakes, or appearing ignorant."[4] Learning requires you periodically eat humble pie and admit you don't have all the answers. Some people never advance because they think they have learned all that is needed to know. Frank Lawrence says this to the know-it-alls, "Anyone who thinks he knows all the answers isn't up to date on the questions."[5] Revive your curiosity by making yourself an expert at asking questions.

Today's organization has no pity on the person who is lackadaisical about learning. People are expected to take responsibility for updating their skills or be left in the dust. Becoming obsolete happens quickly without constant retooling. Your supervisor may be a great advocate for personal growth, but you will ultimately need to jump-start the internal drive to stay abreast of what's needed for you to acquire the necessary specialized knowledge. The more you know, the more valuable you become.

Prepare now to be ready for your inheritance...the future.

> In time of drastic change, it is the learners who inherit the future. The learned usually find themselves equipped to live in a world that no longer exists.
>
> Eric Hoffer[6]

Chapter 6

Grow Beyond Where You Are

Only those who constantly retool themselves stand a chance of staying employed in the years ahead.

Tom Peters[1]

UPDATE YOUR RESUME. LIST ALL of your skills, talents, and unique abilities. Include both your personal and professional qualities. Don't break your arm patting yourself on the back, but do take time to review the achievements you've experienced.

Now, based on what you've written, ask yourself the following question: *What have I done in the past thirty days to increase my competence in these areas and expand my capabilities?*

The one considered the most valuable by employers is an ever-growing, always expanding individual. Think beyond the basics you have mastered. Instead of locking your radar into a comfort zone, pursue the unknown. Gain insight into areas others have overlooked. Become inquisitive by exploring options for improvements.

Resting on past achievements is no longer acceptable and far from guaranteeing a promising career. Constant upgrading of skills is required to face the changing nature of the world around us.

Job security isn't earned by showing up. We need to reformat our thinking around the value we offer to the organization. Feeling entitled to climbing another rung on the ladder, salary increases or even maintaining our present positions is a defeating trap.

Become an expert at what you do. Constant retooling. Perpetual learning. Professional renewal. These are the tools of a marketable and competent professional.

My daughter was a dancer for many years. I marveled at the effort it took for her to achieve new levels of dance precision. Practice involved stretching muscles, coordinating graceful steps and distinct arm movements, pushing her limits, and all the while producing a smile that camouflaged her discomfort.

The year-end dance recital created excitement and anticipation for the performers to display the fruits of their efforts. Grueling hours of instruction and learning culminated into a parent-pleasing production. But none of this is possible without incremental, consistent growth.

Your recital is a daily performance that requires you to dream, dare, stretch, and risk outside the ordinary habitual ambitions. Don't let the past or present competencies evolve into future inadequacies. Work through the discomfort that often accompanies stretching. Remind yourself daily that the more you challenge yourself to expand beyond the customary comfort box, the easier your task will be when called upon to perform a crowd pleasing production.

Excelling requires us to move beyond past limitations and the present status quo. Reinvest your energies in the undiscovered, uncharted, unusual. Create a new performance paradigm that yields a shift in the way you've always approached your job.

The more you know, the more you know how to do, the better you do it, the more valuable you become, and the more career satisfaction you'll attain.

> As long as you're green, you're growing; as soon as you're ripe, you start to rot.
>
> Ray Kroc[2]

Chapter 7

PREPARING FOR THE FUTURE

The pace of events is moving so fast that unless we can find some way to keep our sights on tomorrow, we cannot expect to be in touch with today.

Dean Rusk[1]

YOU CAN'T FORGET YOUR PAST but neither do you have to live in it. Jack Hayford, pastor of Church of the Way in Van Nuys, California, commented, "The past is a dead issue, and we can't gain any momentum moving toward tomorrow if we are dragging the past behind us."[2] As important as your past is, it is not as important as the way you see and prepare for the future. Therefore, our efforts should be directed toward refining our vision, not saving our memory.

Helpful Hints for Building Your Future:

Know what you stand for. I've encountered a lot of people in recent years who are troubled about tomorrow. People worry about what's coming next, especially in these days of uncertainty and change. How can we keep our lives on track?

One anecdote for these anxieties is to know exactly for what you stand. What values and principles guide your life? Where are you willing to be flexible? In what areas is there no room for negotiation? Be clear about the boundaries that will provide a clear path for you to live your life.

Double check your perspective. Where there is no hope in the future, we remain obsessed with the past. Where there is faith in the future, there is power to live today.

Fear is a normal emotion when we look ahead. That's one reason why a lot of people keep living in the past. What's there to fear, I've already endured it all? There are a lot of uncontrollable variables when you begin anticipating tomorrow. But it is tomorrow where we will spend the rest of our lives, and it is unhealthy and unnecessary to let fear remain in control.

There is a definite fascination with pointing out the inevitable downside of the future. It's anti-productive to complain about possible future events. Substantial energy is lost resisting, being angry, or avoiding a future that challenges present assumptions and expectations. Maintain the faith, see the bigger picture, and invest your energies seizing potential opportunities.

Be flexible. Somebody once said, "Blessed are the flexible, for they shall not be bent out of shape."[3] Here's a bit of advice that should go without saying BUT it bears repeating: Be prepared that not everything in life will go according to YOUR plan.

Considerable disappointment could be averted if people would look for new approaches when things don't go their way. Rather than bemoaning the unfairness of life, invest your energy in finding and seizing previously non-existent, priceless opportunities. By catching on to this principle, you'll be better able to remain caught up with the pace of change.

Allow the virtues of hard work and positive anticipation to create a renewed sense of hope for future success.

Focus on a vision for the future. Fasten your seat belt. This step is going to take a fast track to some serious thought control and adjustment. Instead of worrying about or bemoaning all that could happen, get busy creating a vision of the future you want.

Peter Block, in *The Empowered Manager*, reminds us that, "We claim ownership over our lives when we identify the future that we want for ourselves and our unit. Our deepest commitment is to choose to live, to choose the destiny that has been handed to us, and to choose to pursue that destiny. These choices are expressed at work when we create a vision for our unit and decide to pursue that vision at all costs."[4]

You will be far happier if you put the future to work for you rather than allowing the future to work you. Make next week, next year and the coming decade your ally by determining what you want and setting your sights on achieving it. Keep the vision continually in front of you, review it frequently in your imagination, and determine specific actions that will move you closer each day.

André Gide suggested, "One doesn't discover new lands without consenting to lose sight of the shore for a very long time."[5] Put the shore of yesterday behind you and begin stretching for a new horizon.

> Today is the first day of the rest of your life. So, it's no use fussing about the past because you can't do anything about it. But you have today, and today is when everything that's going to happen from now on begins.
>
> Harvey Firestone, Jr.[6]

Chapter 8

SETTLE FOR NOTHING
LESS THAN WOW!

Do what you do so well that those who see you do what you do are going to come back to see you do it again and tell others that they should see what you do.

Walt Disney[1]

ENRY WARD BEECHER BELIEVED THAT to achieve success you need to, "Hold yourself responsible for a higher standard than anybody else expects of you."[2]

"No one ever attains very eminent success by simply doing what is required of him," added Charles Kendall Adams, "it is the amount and excellence of what is over and above the required that determines greatness."[3]

As a young father, Walt Disney would accompany his daughters on a Sunday afternoon get-away to a local amusement park. While sitting on a dirty park bench, indulging in stale popcorn, rubbery hot dogs, and watered-down drinks, he dreamed of creating the ideal amusement park. He dreamed of a place where families around the world would be attracted to visit. From Mainstreet USA to Pirates of the Caribbean, Disney thought through every intricate detail. Quality food, cleanliness, attractive and inviting rides, and a variety of wholesome entertainment would be fun for everyone. This would be a family adventure second to none.

It took Walt fifteen years to make his dream a reality. Even those closest to Disney found it hard to relate to his expansive vision, and his own brother, Roy, thought the entire concept was a screwball idea. Walt encountered numerous obstacles and problems. It would have been easy to settle for something less than the ideal. But by the time Disneyland opened in 1955, the real thing was just as impressive as he had pictured it.

Thirty thousand people visited Disneyland on opening day. By the end of seven weeks, one million people had enjoyed Disney's creation, and now millions of people each year experience the fulfillment of Disney's own admonition: "Do what you do so well that those who see you do what you do are going to come back to see you do it again and tell others that they should see what you do."[4]

Disney knew that if he didn't create a "Wow" experience, people would forget Disneyland existed, and it would soon be considered just another run-of-the-mill amusement park. To avoid such a demise, the brass on Disneyland's carousel is polished daily, the park benches always appear new due to frequent applications of paint, and the shooting gallery targets get a paint touch-up every night. The cleaning crew is extensively trained before assuming their incredible challenge, and even the car parking crew is thoroughly instructed on Disney's commitment to courtesy.

Walt Disney raised the bar on amusement park expectations. He began with a lofty vision of what could be and persevered in selling that vision and the tangible result. Disney paid very close attention to details and challenged developers to continually find ways to improve on the design. His own personal high standards and self-discipline made it possible for those carrying on after him to create a "wow" experience.[4]

You will only be as good as the choices you make. Talent, circumstances, luck, heredity, environment, and personality are immaterial. What matters is how good you plan to be using what you have.

Personal and professional excellence requires 100 percent all the time. A passionate commitment 89, 93, or even 98 percent of the time reduces the "wow" factor to acceptable or mediocre. Adequacy is an unstimulating goal to attain. If you want others to notice your efforts, make plans to do it better than you or they ever thought possible.

"No matter what you do, do it to your utmost," advised Russel H. Conwell. "I always attribute my success...to always requiring myself to do my level best, if only in driving a tack in straight."[5] Enough said.

> My philosophy is that not only are you responsible for your life, but doing the best at this moment puts you in the best place for the next moment.
>
> Oprah Winfrey[6]

Section Three

OWNERSHIP: BECOME THE OWN IN OWNERSHIP

Chapter 9

ACT LIKE AN OWNER

The secret to success on the job is to work as though you were working for yourself. Your company provides you with the work area, equipment and other benefits, but basically you know what has to get done and the best way to do it, so it's up to you to run your own show.

Lair Ribeiro[1]

C ALCULATE THE HOURS YOU SPEND at work, and you'll quickly realize your job represents a major part of your life. It requires a huge investment, so working for just a paycheck and a few benefits will provide only temporary enjoyment. One of the worst mistakes you can make is to think you are working for someone else.

Andy Grove, Intel Corporation's CEO, gave a group of graduates at the University of California in Berkeley some sound advice. He said, "Accept that no matter where you go to work, you are not an employee—you are a business with one employee, you. Nobody owes you a career. You own it, as a sole proprietor. You must compete with millions of individuals every day of your career. You must enhance your value every day, hone your competitive advantage, learn, adapt, move jobs and industries—retrench so you can advance, learn new skills. So you do not become one of those statistics in 2015. And remember: this process starts on Monday."[2]

Activating an Ownership Lifestyle

Assume the presidency of your own personal corporation. Accept responsibility for results. A natural outcome will be that your performance advances to the next level. You are ultimately accountable for the quality of your work. Challenge yourself to do whatever it takes to be successful. No matter who signs your paycheck, in the final analysis, you work for yourself.

Invest yourself passionately in what you do. There is no room in today's marketplace for people who punch in, half-heartedly go through eight hours of repetitive motions, and punch out. Take charge of your morale. Don't depend on the organization or someone else to pump you up. No one possesses the power to keep you inspired. Fill your own energy tank.

Never confuse longevity with contribution. Tenure is important if you continue to add value to your department and/or the organization. I feel sorry for people who live under the mistaken assumption that longevity qualifies them for security, additional salary or added privileges. It just doesn't work that way. Organizations simply don't take the personal interest in people's careers like they did in the past. Most of us are primarily on our own.

Loyalty to your company is valuable but you don't get extra credit for "putting in your time." Look outside your job description to find ways to contribute more to the organization than you cost. Do more than you are asked. Stay later than is expected of you. Search for ways to increase your worth to the organization far beyond what you are being paid. Make it evident that you would be missed if you weren't there.

Think in terms of partnership. J.C. Penney once declared, "I will have no man work for me who has not the capacity to become a partner."[3] Inspire other people to make things happen. Cultivate cooperative relationships. Assume more personal responsibility for the success of the organization. Create a vision of what your department could become. How can you personally cut costs, improve productivity, eliminate waste, serve the customer better, and improve the emotional well-being of the company?

Become a perpetual learner. Organizations need high performance people. It is virtually impossible to stay on the cutting-edge of your profession without continual growth. Become a master at what you do. Stay abreast of what is happening in your field. The choice is to either be a perpetual student who continually acquires new skills or become outdated and obsolete.

Learn to deal with ambiguity and uncertainty. Proactively endorse shifting and expanding responsibilities. Remain fluid and flexible. Improvise as necessary and accept the fact that times are changing and things are not returning to normal. Feel your way down the path to the future and remain answerable for your actions. Become self-empowered. Discover your untapped potential.

Behaving like you're in business for yourself frees you to capitalize on possibilities and be accountable for outcomes. This is a marvelous opportunity to shine in your position, develop an entrepreneurial reputation, and make a significant difference for those who pay for your work.

> Always accept yourself as self-employed and look upon every single thing you accomplish or don't accomplish as your own responsibility.
>
> Brian Tracy[4]

Chapter 10

TAKE THE TIME TO FIX
YOUR LEAKY BOAT

The rule of accuracy: When working toward the solution of a problem it always helps if you know the answer.

John Peer[1]

HERE'S SOME NEWS YOU'LL LOVE to hear: problems are a part of every job. What's important is whether you decide to do something about your problems or just complain about them. It's easy to get so caught up in your trials and tribulations that you fail to get beyond them.

A man in a rowboat, about twenty-five yards off shore, was rowing like crazy but getting nowhere. A woman on shore noticed the rowboat had a bad leak and was slowly sinking. She shouted to the man who was too busy bailing water to answer her. Finally she yelled at the top of her lungs, "Hey, if you don't get the boat ashore and fix the leak, you're going to drown!"

"Thanks, lady," the man replied, "but I don't have time to fix the leak."[2]

We all encounter situations when it takes every ounce of energy we have just to stay afloat. Bailing and rowing become the dominant activities. If we would only take the time to fix the source of our problem, rather than just attacking the symptoms, we might not be so worn out at the end of the day. Every job requires us to go ashore periodically to fix our leaky boats.

Problems happen. You'll see plenty in your career. Build a reputation as a problem-solver, and you'll be considered a valuable person on the team. Here are a few strategies for fixing the leaks:

Admit there is a leak. "Stubbornness in refusing to recognize a problem has destroyed a lot of bottom lines," observed Harvey Mackay. "You can't solve a problem unless you first admit you have one."[3]

In his book *Identity: Youth and Crisis*, Erik Erikson tells a story he got from a physician about a man with a peculiar situation. The old man vomited every morning but had never felt any inclination to consult a doctor. Finally, the man's family convinced him to get checked out.

The doctor asked, "How are you?"

"I'm fine," the man responded. "Couldn't be better."

The doctor examined him and found he was in good shape for his age. Finally, the physician grew impatient and asked, "I hear that you vomit every morning."

The old man looked surprised and said, "Sure. Doesn't everybody?"[4]

Some people have been dealing with the same problem for so long they've convinced themselves that everyone has a leaky boat. "Recognizing a problem doesn't always bring a solution," James Baldwin reminds us, "but until we recognize that problem, there can be no solution."[5]

Be realistic about the size of the hole. Many times people look at a problem telescopically so the leak looks bigger than it actually is. American publisher Al Neuharth said, "The difference between a mountain and a molehill is your perspective."[6]

A businessperson experienced a drastic downturn in sales, and the possibility of shutting down was a real threat. When asked how he was doing, the man replied, "Times are so tough I'm getting several calls a day from national leaders."

The friend was taken back a bit and asked, "Why are they calling you?"

The down-in-the-mouth executive replied, "They enjoy talking with someone who has bigger problems than they do."[7]

John Maxwell believes, "People need to change their perspectives, not their problems."[8] Don't exaggerate the enormity of your problems. Overreacting or "catastrophizing" puts the power in the problem rather than your ability to solve it.

Don't wait for a lifeguard. Accept responsibility for the problems you are experiencing and you can begin to rise above the crisis. Wait for a lifeguard to rescue you, and you may drown before help arrives.

A critical mistake many people make is assigning fault for a problem and then removing themselves from any responsibility for resolving it. If you're in the boat and the boat springs a leak, whose problem is it? Even though the leak might have been created by someone else, it would be wise for you to make some adjustments or be willing to accept the annoyances, conflict, or drowning the leak will cause.

Because we've gotten so good at the blame game and avoiding personal responsibility, we've become victims by our own choices. Comedian and actor W.C. Fields said, "Remember, a dead fish can float downstream, but it takes a live one to swim upstream."[9] It takes minimal effort or skill to point an accusing finger at other people. What difference does it make now to blame others? The problem is yours and is in need of corrective action.

The effective person is the one who can navigate upstream, against the flow of irresponsibility and finger-pointing, toward workable solutions. It's your boat. Take ownership for its condition. Don't focus on the leak. That only produces fear, anger, desperation or paralysis. Trapped in those emotional reactions, the clarity of the ideal solution is blurred. Tap into your experience and insight to discover how best to solve the leak.

Find a plug that fills the hole. The epitome of frustration comes from the continual analysis of a problem without a proper diagnosis and plan of action. You can stare at a hole in the boat and repeat to yourself over and over, "Yep, there's a hole in the boat," but until a course of correction is set, this risk of sinking remains. John Foster Dulles, Secretary of State during the Eisenhower administration, suggested that, "The measure of success is not whether you have a tough problem to deal with but whether it's the same problem you had last year."[10]

A.B. Simpson told the story of a farmer who plowed around a large rock in his field year after year. He had broken several pieces of equipment by running into it. Each time he saw the rock sprawled out in his field, he grumbled about how much trouble it had caused.

One day the farmer decided to dig up the rock and do away with it for good. Putting a large crowbar under one side, he began prying and soon discovered, much to his surprise, that the rock was less than a foot thick. Within a short period of time, he had removed the rock from the field and hauled it away in his wagon. He smiled to think how that "monstrous" rock had caused him so much frustration.[11]

Quit plowing around your problems. They will still be there tomorrow. We don't need the same old problems reoccurring day after day after day. New challenges are continually coming your way and the cumulative affect of new and old problems can be overwhelming.

Dispose of the old hassles. Take care of them so you can move on to new opportunities.

Understand the value of leaks. Problems are a natural, inevitable condition for growth. All growth produces problems but not all problems produce growth. The difference is your understanding of that truth. Lloyd Ogilvie, writing in his book *If God Cares, Why Do I Still Have Problems,* suggests, "The greatest problem we all share, to a greater or lesser degree, is a profound misunderstanding of the positive purpose of problems. Until we grapple with this gigantic problem, we will be helpless victims of our problems all through our life."[12]

Problems are a source of instruction, insight and opportunity. The challenge of facing those problems keeps us vibrant and on our toes. Problems stimulate our development while stretching our thinking and performance. Resenting or avoiding problems keeps us from experiencing the benefits they can bring.

In *The Road Less Traveled*, best-selling author Scott Peck offers this valuable perspective on problems:

> It is in this whole process of meeting and solving problems that life has meaning. Problems are the cutting edge that distinguishes between success and failure. Problems call forth our courage and our wisdom; indeed they create our courage and our wisdom. It is only because of problems that we grow mentally and spiritually. It is through the pain of confronting and resolving problems that we learn. As Benjamin Franklin said, "Those things that hurt, instruct."[13]

Look for the value in each challenge. Every miracle in the Bible began with a problem. So, when you find yourself surrounded by water in your leaking boat, implement the suggestions you've read. You're a candidate for a miracle.

> The best way to eat the elephant standing in your path is to cut it up into little pieces.
>
> African Proverb[14]

Chapter 11

DON'T HOLD BACK

There's a difference between interest and commitment. When you're interested in doing something, you do it only when it is convenient. When you are committed to something, you accept no excuses, only results.

Kenneth H. Blanchard[1]

SOME PEOPLE WILL ALWAYS EMBRACE Mark Twain's attitude when he said, "I do not like work even when someone else does it."[2] However, I'm convinced that most of us are interested in erasing any possibility for a vague and undefined work life. The simple fact is we want more than a paycheck.

I predict there are very few people in the world who get up in the morning, shower, dress, have a little breakfast, and announce, "I can't wait to do a really BAD job today."

Yet, surveys indicate nearly 85 percent of the workers in the United States say they could work harder on the job; nearly half claim they could double their effectiveness.

Too many people are not emotionally committed to the importance of what they do. The job is often blamed, but that is absurd. For every person complaining about his job, there are several others investing themselves in those perceived mundane experiences.

Every organization has people who always do less than they are told, others who will do only what they are told, and some who will do things without being told. What organizations need more of is the minority group who actually inspire others to do things. These are people who constantly renew their own commitment to being their best.

The world has little room for people who put in their time, go through the motions with a half-hearted effort, and are careless, sloppy, or even indifferent. In today's world, people who eliminate excuses, proactively work from the heart, invest themselves passionately in what they do, and apply their skills and talents to the fullest are maximizing their professional potential.

President Eisenhower, while addressing the National Press Club, opened his remarks by apologizing that he was not a great orator. He likened his situation to a boyhood experience on a Kansas farm. Eisenhower recalled,

> An old farmer had a cow that we wanted to buy. We went over to visit him and asked about the cow's pedigree. The old farmer didn't know what pedigree meant, so we asked him about the cow's butterfat production. He told us that he hadn't any idea. Finally, we asked him if he knew how many pounds of milk the cow produced each year. The farmer shook his head and said, "I don't know. But she's an honest old cow and she'll give you all the milk she has!"

Eisenhower then concluded his opening remarks, "Well, I'm like the cow: I'll give you everything I have."[3]

That is a pure and simple commitment. When the urge to slough off arises or you're on the verge of giving less than your best, consider Eisehower's pledge. Giving everything you have makes work far more satisfying. It's a great anecdote for boredom.

> Commitment unlocks the doors of imagination, allows vision and gives us the 'right stuff' to turn our dreams into reality.
>
> James Womack[4]

Chapter 12

MAKING A DIFFERENCE

You have not lived a perfect day, even though you have earned your money, unless you have done something for someone who will never be able to repay you.

Ruth Smeltzer[1]

I REMEMBER ENJOYING A WONDERFUL FALL conference. The feeling of family was definitely evident in everything we did. Each year the home office and facility team members become more and more like "family." The feelings of "us versus them" diminish. People genuinely care about each other. It is heart warming to observe, experience, and reflect on what that means to the company.

My trip home from conference was filled with positive reflections, a grateful heart, and an enthusiastic anticipation for the future.

Immediately upon arriving home on a Friday evening, I began pecking out a fall conference reflection email to those who attended.

My home phone rang.

"Van Ekeren's," I answered.

"Is this Glenn Van Ekeren?"

"Yes it is."

"Is this the same Glenn Van Ekeren who worked at Cran Hill Ranch 35 years ago?"

"Yes??"

"Do you remember Cindi and Linda?"

"Absolutely! Cindi Callan and Linda Vander Woude."

"That's right. I can't believe you remember. I'm Linda."

Go back in time with me thirty-five years (some of you aren't old enough to do that, but try anyway). I worked ten weeks one summer at a church camp in Big Rapids, Michigan called Cran Hill Ranch. It was a fabulous camp environment in a secluded, forest-like setting. It was perfect for the kids from the "city" who couldn't wait to get away from mom and dad for a week.

Although I was normally a counselor for about fifteen young boys (sleeping in one large tent), for some reason I became especially close to Linda and Cindi. They were both cuter than a bug's ear and had delightful, endearing personalities. We migrated to each other and I was sad to see them go home. It was amazing how close we became in five short days.

Back in college, I received an unexpected call late winter from Michigan informing me that Cindi had cancer and was going to have one leg amputated. No way! No thirteen-year-old girl should have to lose a leg. Besides, in 1972 we didn't know much about this dreadful six letter word—cancer. Only old people got cancer and even then I had no idea why.

I was devastated. I felt absolutely helpless. I was fifteen hours away from Wyoming, Michigan where she lived (even driving well over the speed limit) and frankly this is a young lady I had only known for one week.

I shared my heart with a couple of buddies, and in two days we arranged a trip to Michigan over our Easter break. Both girls' parents were hesitant, to say the least (you would be too if you saw pictures of these three long haired, scruffy looking college kids) to have these unknown college "boys" come see their little girls. They finally agreed to let us come if they were with us all the time. We drove all night and arrived in Wyoming, Michigan, late on Friday morning.

What a weekend. The emotions, silence, laughter, prayers, tears, pizza, and most of all memories created were deeply embedded. Cindi's positive attitude about her loss, the unknown future challenges, and the ugly disease impacted my young, immature 20-year-old mind. Linda's commitment to her teen-age friend made an indelible impression as well.

I kept the pictures of that weekend until last winter. I finally decided keeping and periodically looking at the pictures didn't make me feel any younger so I discarded them. But the mental pictures are as vivid as the brilliant blue sky in the Midwest on a summer day.

Back to September 12, 2008, and the phone call.

"Glenn, Cindi and I had lunch today and were reminiscing about your visit to Wyoming, Michigan, for that short weekend right after her surgery. You will never know what that meant to us, and I'm just calling thirty-five years later to let you know."

Never, never, never underestimate the little things you do for people and the potential impact your act of kindness can have on their lives. In business, moving toward success includes acts of kindness in small things. Maybe, just for today, we can all find a way to do less paperwork and instead seek out ways to make a difference in someone's life.

What the world needs is more love and less paperwork.

Pearl Bailey[2]

Investment: Give Your Best To What Matters Most

Chapter 13

Take a Few Minutes to Think About Time

Time only runs in one direction and seems to do so in an orderly fashion.

Patricia Cornwell[1]

Bernard Berenson once commented, "I wish I could stand on a busy corner, hat in hand, and beg people to throw me all their wasted hours."[2] There's a good chance he'd become a wealthy man given the opportunity to fulfill his wish. I doubt there is anything people waste more of than time.

Time management expert Michael Fortino launched an in-depth study called the Fortino Efficiency Index. Fortino discovered that during the course of a lifetime, the average American spends...

- One year looking for misplaced objects
- Eight months opening junk mail
- Two years trying to return phone calls of people who never seem to be in

- Five years standing in line (at the bank, movie theater, etc.)[3]

Additional research by Tor Dahl, Chairman of the World Confederation of Productivity Science, indicates that the average American business wastes or misdirects work time as follows:

- 23 percent waiting for approvals, materials or support
- 20 percent doing things that shouldn't even be done
- 15 percent doing things that should be handled by someone else
- 18 percent by doing things wrong
- 16 percent for failure to do the right things[4]

Sound familiar? You can list additional daily activities in our instant message, text, cyberspace, and beaming world that rob valuable time.

My intent is not to offer a cure-all for the epidemic of lost time. I am offering you an assorted selection of antibiotics you can draw on to treat this infection. Although our lack of effectiveness and efficiency can be hindered by a number of external infecting agents, we are ultimately responsible for dealing with the causes and symptoms. Time is your personal possession. Nobody can manage it or fix it for you. Your life is yours; you can choose to live it with greater control and healthy use of time.

You might be plagued with a lack of self discipline, indecisiveness or personal disorganization. Maybe time slips by through daydreaming, poor delegation skills, an inability to say no, or a lack of priorities. Whatever the case, here is a plethora of ideas for you to consider. Give immediate attention to those that cause an "Aha" reaction.

1. Ask the right question. First and foremost, when involved in any activity that hints of wasted time, ask yourself, "Is this the best way for me to be spending my time right now?" Then, act accordingly.

2. Schedule work according to your peak productivity time. Designate those hours you are most productive to doing things that give the highest return and produce the greatest value. The German poet Goethe put it this way: "The key to life is concentration and elimination."[5]

3. Determine your priorities. You can't do everything. Overly ambitious to-do lists can be unrealistic and anti-productive. Make choices. Sort out your "have-to's" from your "choose-to's." Direct your energies toward activities that are the most important to you.

Robert Eliot suggested,

> It's important to run not on the fast track, but on your track. Pretend you only have six months to live, and make three lists: The things you have to do, want to do, and neither have to do nor want to do. Then, for the rest of your life, forget everything on the third list.[6]

4. Be result oriented rather than activity oriented. Activity does not equal accomplishment. "No other principle of effectiveness is violated as constantly today as the basic principle of concentration," said Peter Drucker. "Our motto seems to be, 'let's do a little bit of everything.'"[7] Measure your effectiveness by what you achieve not by how busy you are.

5. Get organized. According to Albert R. Karr, writing in the *Wall Street Journal*, "Executives waste nearly six weeks a year looking for misplaced items, according to a poll of two hundred large-company executives for Accountemps, a temporary help firm."[8] Have a place for everything, and have everything in its place.

6. Get up earlier. By rising thirty minutes earlier each day, you add three and a half hours of productivity to your week. Multiply that by fifty-two weeks and you'll have an additional 180 hours to accomplish your priorities. I've used these extra hours to write books, design seminars, and get energized spiritually by reading inspirational material or spending time in prayer.

7. Learn to say no. Busy people must learn to refuse some demands made on their time. It's natural not to want to disappoint people. Sometimes we're unrealistic about our limits. It's easy to let our ego get in the way of saying no; the need to be needed is a powerful decision influence. Nicely, just say no.

8. Work on your attitude. Your attitude about how busy you are, the amount of time you have, or the demands on your life, can sabotage any effort to make the most of the time. Be flexible. Not everything will go as expected. When your game plan runs into road blocks, seek new opportunities.

9. Quit daydreaming. Turn mind wandering into action.

10. Do things right the first time. If you don't have time to do it right, you won't have time to do it over.

11. Plan ahead. Lay your clothes out for the next day before you go to bed. Purchase holiday or birthday presents early. Keep tabs on special events thirty days in advance.

12. Place deadlines on yourself. Don't allow minor or major projects to drag on indefinitely. Challenge yourself with deadlines, and beat them.

13. Prepare for unexpected down time. Spare minutes created by waiting in airports, restaurants, traffic, etc. can be perfect moments to indulge in small projects.

14. Manage meetings. Use specific time like 9:13 or 1:32 to start your meetings and set a predetermined time for adjournment. Stay on task.

15. Don't put off until the day after tomorrow what you can do today. Procrastination is an ugly habit. Do it today.

The philosopher and poet Goethe said, "We have time enough if we will but use it aright."[9] Time is a precious commodity. It is available to all of us in equal parts to use as we choose. Savor each moment. Make the most of every hour. Time is like a talent—you can't produce more of it but you can make the most of what you have.

> I would rather be ashes than dust! I would rather that my spark should burn out in a brilliant blaze than it should be stifled by dry rot. I would rather be a superb meteor, every atom of me in magnificient glow, than a sleepy and permanent planet. The proper function of man is to live, not to exist. I shall not spend my days trying to prolong them. I shall use my time.
>
> Jack London[10]

Chapter 14

LEARN TO SCHEDULE
YOUR PRIORITIES

*The reason most major goals are not achieved is that we spend
our time doing second things first.*

Robert McKain[1]

NOTICE THE TITLE DOESN'T READ "prioritize your schedule."
Instead, decide what you want to spend your time doing.
What are the most important elements of your life and
work? Establish your priorities, schedule them, and stick to them.

Unless you live congruently with your priorities, you'll always
have that nagging feeling that you're in a rat race you can't win.
Awareness of and commitment to our priorities increases performance and productivity. With forces pulling us in every direction,
this principle is more important than ever.

Allow sufficient time and energy to enjoy what you value most.
This is the simplest yet most profound foundation for a successful
life. All other goals and strategies for attaining them will fall into
place when you live by the values you profess.

Don't be driven by distractions. Jumping from one thing to the next is the result of an undisciplined commitment to priorities. You don't have the emotional or physical energy to sufficiently support every worthy ideal vying for your attention.

Each day we are given the gift of 24 hours, 1,440 minutes, 86,400 seconds. Only one person can decide how this gift will be used. How we decide to invest our time communicates to others the values we espouse. Ponder this question for a few days: "Am I satisfied with the amount and quality of time I am giving to the important priorities in my life?"

Whenever we decide to do one thing, we have made a decision not to give our attention to something else. Time management, or life management, is a series of choices.

My fascination with the circus led me to discover the secret of the lion tamer's success. I found that, along with the whip and pistol strapped to his belt, the lion tamer's key tool is a four-legged stool. The stool is held by the back and the legs are thrust toward the face of the lion. Apparently the wild animal attempts to focus on all four legs at once, thereby overwhelming its senses. The lion is left paralyzed, tamed, and unable to aggressively respond. Sound familiar? Focus. Focus. Focus.

What are the top five personal priorities in your life? What are your five most important professional responsibilities? How much time have you given to each in the past six months? Are the hours and days adding up to the quality of life you desire?

If sufficient time and energy have been allocated for these priorities, you probably sense a degree of balance. If, on the other hand, these priorities are pushed on the back burner, I would wager there is a feeling of incompleteness and dissatisfaction.

Please note the wording of this strategy. I'm not suggesting a prioritizing of all daily responsibilities and events. Rather, based on your purpose, determine your top personal and professional priorities. Now schedule them into your weekly calendar. Make sure these priorities are given top billing.

Most people don't have trouble listing their priorities. Few people seem to be able to give sufficient time to them. We have good intentions. We make a gallant effort for a few weeks, but then fall back into the habit of allowing our calendars to dictate our priorities. Soon life is out of sync.

I'm involved in a greenhouse operation that raises twenty-eight hundred tomato plants. For us to raise the highest quality tomatoes takes considerable maintenance. Little shoots at the bottom of the plant must be trimmed or they will drain nutrients from the main stem. By trimming the "suckers," the remainder of the plant receives proper nourishment, thereby producing luscious fruit.

Our automatic watering system insures each plant receives sufficient moisture to keep it healthy. Without the water, the plants would shrivel up and die. We have the labor and nutritional resources to support each plant.

Snip off your time suckers. Let them go. Nourish the fruit producing priorities. Give them your energetic attention and celebrate the results. Put into action today a plan that will allow you to choose how the precious gift of time will be spent.

> Things that matter most must never be at the mercy of things that matter least.
>
> Johann Wolfgang von Goethe[2]

Chapter 15

I Know You're Busy, But What are You Getting Done?

Do not tell me how hard you work. Tell me how much you get done.

James J. Ling[1]

O̶UR HIGH SCHOOL SPANISH CLUB sold candy to raise money for a trip to Mexico. The sponsoring teacher reminded each student how important it was for them to contact as many people as possible about buying the candy. "We've got ten days to make this fund-raiser successful," the teacher instructed. "I want to know at the end of those ten days how many contacts you made. Good luck."

As the students brought in their orders, one girl was bragging about her success. "Well, tell us about it," the teacher encouraged. "I called on seventy-four houses door-to-door in one night. I started right after school and didn't even stop for supper. I would have been able to do more but a couple of people stopped me and wanted to buy."

In our fast-paced world it is easy to get caught up in a fury of activity. Observe people around you as they're attending one meeting after another, attempting to concentrate on several activities or projects at one time, writing reports, talking on the phone while emailing, eating on the run, and accomplishing very little.

The world doesn't care how busy you are. The world doesn't reward you for how smart you are, your good intentions, or the dreams you hope to pursue.

What's important? Results. Far too often, we pat ourselves on the back for running in place even though the finish line is as far away at the end of the day as when we started the day. People who get things done will reap more than a self-appreciating pat on the back.

Making the transformation involves an evaluation of current activity. Henry Ford said, "The number of needless tasks that are performed daily by thousands of people is amazing."[2] He had a list of them including:

- They make too many phone calls.
- They visit too often and stay too long on each visit.
- They write letters that are three times as long as necessary.
- They work on little things, neglect big ones.
- They read things that neither inform nor inspire them.
- They have too much fun, too often.
- They spend hours with people who cannot stimulate them.
- They read every word of advertising circulars.
- They pause to explain why they did what they did, when they should be working on the next thing.
- They hurry to the movies when they should be going to night school.
- They daydream at work when they should be planning ahead for their job.

- They spend time and energy on things that don't count.

Sound a bit harsh? They are worthy guidelines, however, when we get caught in the activity trap. No one feels like being productive every day. But a bit more focus might result in substantial fulfillment.

Forget your excuses, lack of energy, and obsession with being busy. Do the things you know you have to do to achieve the results you want to achieve, and become the person you want to be.

> A fellow doesn't last long on what he has done. He's got to keep on delivering as he goes along.
>
> Carl Hubbell[3]

Chapter 16

TAKE YOUR JOB AND LOVE IT!

Are you bored with life? Then throw yourself into some work you believe in with all your heart. Live for it, die for it, and you will find happiness that you had thought could never be yours.

Dale Carnegie[1]

WHY DO SOME PEOPLE SEEM to enjoy their jobs more than others? Warren Buffet was addressing a group of college students. Unsurprisingly, they wanted to know the key to his success. His response surprised a few of the curious Buffet "wannabes." "If there is a difference between you and me," he said, "it may simply be that I get up every day and have a chance to do what I love to do every day. If you want to learn anything from me, this is the best advice I can give you."[2]

When work, commitment and pleasure come together and are accented by passion, the possibilities are limitless. And the best part of it all is that the satisfaction, fun, and fulfillment we experience in work are benefits we can give ourselves.

Maybe we could benefit from rethinking our approach to work, starting with three important factors: ability, attitude, and behavior.

Ability. Many people possess latent abilities and unused talents. Unused talents may soon become rusty, antiquated, or even misplaced and lost forever. Using our abilities to the fullest will expand those talents and produce additional opportunities to use them.

Keep in mind, as Leo F. Buscaglia reminds us, "Your talent is God's gift to you. What you do with it is your gift back to God."[3] Find a way to use your unique abilities in a way you've never thought of.

Attitude. Many people truly find "work" to be a four-letter word. It's the unfortunate evil assigned to those desiring a comfortable lifestyle. Ronald Reagan quipped, "It's true hard work never killed anybody, but I figure, why take the chance?"[4] Although intended humorously, the sad reality is that many people have endorsed this approach.

B.C. Forbes wrote: "Whether we find pleasure in our work or whether we find it a bore depends entirely on our mental attitude toward it, not on the task itself."[5] Try for just one day to see everything in your job in a positive light. No matter what, choose an attitude that life just doesn't get much better than this. I think you'll be pleasantly surprised at the outcomes.

Behavior. Industrialist Andrew Carnegie said, "The average person puts only 25 percent of their energy and ability into their work. The world takes off its hat to those who put in more than 50 percent of their capacity, and stands on its head for those few-and-far-between souls who devote 100 percent."[6] Author Bob Biehl adds: "If you are doing what you want to do, you will arrive early and stay late. On the other hand, if your job is something that you do not want to do, you will show up late and leave early."[7]

Interestingly enough, burned out people are not those who work too hard. Burned out people are those who work without a passion or purpose in what they do. Pouring ourselves and our energies into tasks that we know make a difference will minimize the potential of getting bored, bruised, or burned out by our work.

Will Rogers said, "In order to succeed, you must *know* what you are doing, *like* what you are doing, and *believe* in what you are doing."[8] His suggestions deserve a closer look.

1. Know what you are doing. Winners are willing to do the things losers refuse to do. They develop the knowledge, skills, and abilities to rise above mediocre performance to become masters.

As Martin Luther King, Jr. said, "If you are called to be a street sweeper, sweep streets even as Michelangelo painted, or Beethoven composed music, or Shakespeare wrote poetry. Sweep streets so well that all the host of heaven and earth will pause to say, 'Here lived a great street sweeper who did his job well.'"[9]

2. Like what you are doing. I'm baffled by people who spend five days a week doing something they don't like so they can spend the other two days doing what they enjoy. Sister Mary Lauretta said, "To be successful, the first thing to do is fall in love with your work."[10]

The secret to happiness, success, satisfaction, and fulfillment in our work is not doing what one likes, but in liking what one does.

3. Believe in what you do. Successful people are not in a job for something to do; they are in their work to do something, to make a difference. To love what you do and know that it matters is the foundation for believing in what you do.

Get beyond the job description, title, paycheck, or "to do" list. See the end result. Become absorbed with your organization's purpose and mission. Espouse a set of values that demonstrate a conviction for what you do.

The self-esteem, satisfaction, and fulfillment you experience at work depends on you. To transform your daily "have-to's" into a lifestyle of "want-to's," consider these two questions: *"What do I want out of my life's work?"* and, *"What am I willing to do to make it happen?"*

If you love what you do, you'll never have to work another day in your life.

> Few people are lacking in capacity, but they fail because they are lacking in application.
>
> Calvin Coolidge[11]

Section Five

ABILITY: TAP INTO YOUR TALENT

Chapter 17

Focus on What You Do Best

If a man has a talent and cannot use it, he has failed. If he has a talent and uses only half of it, he has partly failed. If he has a talent and learns somehow to use the whole of it, he has gloriously succeeded and won a satisfaction and a triumph few men ever know.

Thomas Wolfe[1]

AN AGENCY REP WAS PRESENTED the challenge of coming up with a campaign to boost the sales of a popular laundry soap. The product had enjoyed strong customer approval for many years. What more could be said that hadn't already been discovered by users?

One day he poured a box of the soap on the top of his desk, hoping to discover something that would prompt his creativity. Suddenly, he noticed the soap was full of little blue crystals. He immediately went to the manufacturer to find out what the blue crystals were all about. What he learned sparked a successful campaign, significantly increasing sales. The blue crystals supplied the soap with super-whitening, brightening agents that made the soap so effective.

Maybe you remember the ad pitch: "Try Tide—With the New Blue Crystals."[2] Even though the crystals had always been there, it wasn't until their purpose and effectiveness was exposed that Tide received recognition for its super cleaning powers.

I work with people every day who are like Tide. Contained inside of them is an important element whose unique value has not been exposed. They are good at what they do but, if they ever realize the latent abilities waiting to be discovered, significant achievements await them. There are gifts waiting to be opened and used.

Excellence is touched when gifts are discovered, activated and continually repeated. How else can we explain the repeated achievements of basketball great Michael Jordan, country music star Garth Brooks, best-selling novelist Tom Clancy, actress Julia Roberts, golfer Tiger Woods, or a host of other less renowned successful people? Achievers have learned to identify and develop their talents by seeking opportunities to use them. Their efforts are concentrated on practicing, enjoying, and refining the gifts they have discovered.

What does this mean for people like us? Everyone is created with the equal ability to become an unequal. Although we're not all created equal, each of us possesses the capacity to stand out from the crowd in some area. One of the basic elements of success is to be good at what you do. You won't be good at what you do unless you polish your skills and perfect your moves. Master the talents you possess. Be determined to live as a "will be" not a "has been."

On Tuesday, April 18, 1995, sports fans around the country had to be a bit saddened to watch superstar Joe Montana retire from professional football after sixteen seasons. Twenty thousand fans gathered in downtown San Francisco for the retirement ceremonies.

Sportscasters, coaches, and players offered their accolades to one of the league's greatest quarterbacks. However, it wasn't always like this. When Joe Montana was recruited as a third-round draft pick out of Notre Dame, San Francisco fans were less than impressed. Montana was labeled with a variety of unflattering labels.

In an answer to his critics, Joe Montana entered the league and quickly began throwing passes with perfect timing. He redefined the two-minute drill. To those who said he was too weak and scrawny to play in the big leagues, he endured season after season of physical abuse. Then, he simply went on to lead the 49er's to four Super Bowls and helped them become a feared and dominant team in the 1980's.[3]

Joe Montana will never be considered a "has been" because of his deliberate commitment to be what he "could be." Montana initially impressed very few people, but his consistent commitment to focus on what he could do best landed him in the record books and earned him the respect of the fans.

To experience ongoing happiness and success with your career, find that talent that brings you joy and fulfillment.

Erica Jong believed that, "Everyone has talent. What is rare is the courage to follow the talent to the dark place where it leads."[4] That dark place is usually unfamiliar and sometimes, unfriendly territory. Go there anyway. Push yourself to develop your talent beyond any level you may have achieved in the past.

> You might say that a peak performer is a person exploring the farther reaches of his or her abilities.
>
> Charles Garfield[5]

Chapter 18

ACHIEVEMENT HAS
NO FINISH LINE

Not once have I heard a peak performer speak of an end to challenge, excitement, curiosity, and wonder. Quite the contrary.
One of their most engaging characteristics is an infectious
talent for moving into the future, generating new challenges,
living with a sense of work to be done.

Dr. Charles Garfield[1]

ACHIEVERS POSSESS A DEDICATION TO action that continually expands their potential and increases their value.
Such a lifestyle requires a commitment beyond what most
people are willing to make.

John Wesley committed 64 years of his life to being an uncommon
achiever for God. He had no interest in being better than other
preachers—he just tended to the business of being his best.

Wesley preached 42,400 sermons, averaging 15 sermons per
week for 54 years. He traveled 290,000 miles (equal to circling
the globe 20 times) on foot or on horseback. No jet services were
available to whisk him across the miles. Travel, combined with his

speaking schedule was a true test of endurance. He was a prolific author. Wesley's works, including translations, amounted to over 200 volumes. When John Wesley died, at age 88, it is said he left a worn coat, a battered hat, a humble cottage, a tattered Bible, and the Methodist Church.[2]

Wesley never considered himself as "having arrived." New sermons, spiritually hungry people, inspired vision, and the internal drive to serve captured his energy. Although the summary of your life might seem minuscule compared to John Wesley, what you can do is achieve a little more today that you did yesterday. Work tomorrow to exceed yesterday's expectations.

Personal achievement has no finish line. As milestones are attained, encouraging you to continue on, remain cautious of the temptation to put your life in neutral. Mediocrity, boredom, and uninspired standards will ultimately creep in and infect you.

Set higher standards for achievement than anyone around you. Compete with yourself to attain higher levels of performance. Unless you undertake more than you can possibly do, you will never do all you can do. This is a critical step to ongoing self-improvement that will jump-start your attitude and increase results. Self-directed pressure keeps you excited and energetic and eager to attain heightened levels of performance.

Mister achievement himself, Thomas Edison, once said, "Three great essentials to achieve anything worthwhile are, first, hard work; second, stick-to-itiveness; third, common sense."[3]

We've talked about hard work. What about stick-to-itiveness? George Bernard Shaw waited nine long years before he got anything published. Editors kept turning down everything he submitted. Undaunted by rejection, Shaw persistently kept working, writing, submitting, believing, and hoping. He also kept getting better at writing and ultimately got something published.

Zig Ziglar, commenting on Shaw's experience, had this observation:

Several factors are important...Shaw believed that he had ability. He patiently persisted in honing his skills and pursuing publishers until finally somebody said yes. That's a good procedure to follow. If you really believe in what you're doing and have confidence that it is significant, you persist until something positive happens, knowing that it's always darkest just before the dawn.[4]

It's easy to get fired up about a dream or goal for a short period of time. Sustaining passion in the face of adversity, rejection or failure is the stuff that achievers are made of. Studies indicate that the one quality all successful people have is persistence. Joyce Brothers sees successful people as, "willing to spend more time accomplishing a task and to persevere in the face of many difficult odds. There's a very positive relationship between people's ability to accomplish any task and the time they're willing to spend on it."[5] The power to press on in spite of everything, the power to endure— this is the achiever's quality. Persistency is the ability to face defeat, challenges and disappointments again and again without giving up—to push on, knowing that you can attain your dreams, or at least a portion of them. Be willing to take the pains to overcome every obstacle, and to do whatever it takes.

The most vivid regrets in my life are those times when I quit too soon. A perceived lack of confidence, energy, or talent caused me to give up without realizing the fulfillment of a plan. I've since realized that any fulfillment worth its salt requires me to do the tough stuff first and realize satisfaction or reward might be down the road. Even when the odds are stacked against me, I've learned to overcome them by sustaining the best effort I know how.

Hang in there! Make stick-to-itiveness your ally.

Edison's recommendation for common sense can't be taught. It is attained only through the practical lessons learned by every day living. People who glean information from their life experiences refine their sense of what works and what doesn't.

Thoughtfully progress down the road to your ultimate goals. Hastiness, reckless pursuit, ignoring stop signs, and illogical turns rarely pay off. Stay the course. Make decisions based on the experiences you've endured.

Achievement may have no finish line but achievers cross the line of short term reward into a lifestyle of challenge and gratification. Every day recharges their spirits and catapults them into new ventures to enjoy.

> What this country needs is dirtier fingernails and cleaner minds.
>
> Will Rogers[6]

Chapter 19

DIG A LITTLE DEEPER

Few people during their lifetime come anywhere near exhausting the resources dwelling within them. There are deep wells of strength that are never used.

Rear Admiral Richard Byrd[1]

T HE TIME WAS THE GREAT Depression. The place was a sheep ranch in Texas. The owner, Mr. Yates, was on the brink of bankruptcy when an oil company, believing there might be oil on his land, asked for permission to drill.

Desperate, feeling he had nothing to lose, Mr. Yates agreed to their request. A short time later, just below the surface, the oil drillers discovered the largest oil deposit found at that time on the North American continent. Overnight, Mr. Yate's financial difficulties disappeared. He was a billionaire.[2]

The amazing thing about this account is that the untapped wealth was there all along. He just didn't realize it.

Now, let's take this illustration a bit further. Alfred Armand Montapert, writing in *The Superior Philosophy of Man*, offered additional insight. He wrote:

In Texas, years ago, almost all of the oil came from surface operations. Then someone got the idea that there were greater sources of supply deeper down. A well was drilled five thousand feet deep. The result? A gusher. Too many of us operate on the surface. We never go deep enough to find the supernatural resources. The result is: we never operate at our best. More time and investment is involved to go deep but a gusher will pay off.[3]

How deep have you dug? How long have you been dependent on surface abilities and talents? Have you tapped your inner supply of energy and potential? Are you satisfied with being an underachiever rather than being committed to maximum achieving? Have you become complacent, doing the same things, in the same way, with the same people, every day? Are you going to get any better or is this as good as it gets?

Successful and unsuccessful people do not vary significantly in what they are capable of doing. There is a giant chasm between successful and unsuccessful people in their desire to stretch and reach toward their potential. Brian Tracy believes,

> Your remarkable and unusual combination of education, experience, knowledge, problems, successes, difficulties, and challenges, and your way of looking at and reacting to life, make you extraordinary. You have within you potential competencies and attributes that can enable you to accomplish virtually anything you want in life. Your main job is to decide which of your talents you're going to exploit and develop to their highest and best possible use right now.[4]

Digging Deeper Devices

1. Think at a higher level. Og Mandino observed, "Your only limitations are those you set up in your mind, or permit others to set up for you."[5]

Digging deep toward your inner potential means expanding your mental boundaries. If you keep plowing around mental obstacles, you'll never discover potential wealth below the surface. Think beyond present constraints. Learn to see what isn't immediately evident. Don't limit your capabilities by what you currently see. Give yourself permission to dig to the next level. What you discover will determine what gets accomplished. Each time you determine, in the privacy of your mind, to cast aside limitations, your capacity to grow and perform dramatically expands.

The person you think you are is the person you will be.

2. Perform at a higher level. My hunting enthusiast friends tell me there is much to learn from ducks. There are two kinds of ducks: puddle ducks and divers. Puddle ducks such as Mallards, Redheads and Mud Hens find pleasure in paddling around the edge of ponds, marshes and lakes. They feed in shallow waters and eat only what they can reach from the surface. Diver ducks, on the other hand, are able to dive to incredible depths in a lake to feed from the plants at the bottom. Mergansers and Canvasbacks are representative of this group. Some divers can go to depths of 150 feet for their food.

Their talk of puddle ducks and divers is a direct correlation to the different types of people. There are people who are consistently satisfied with experiences, achievements, and nourishment found in easy tasks and just being good enough at what they do. Diver people go out on a limb. They look for adventurous opportunities to test their limits and pursue situations that will not only tap but enhance their potential.

Sounds simple, doesn't it? Becoming the best you can be means continually raising the performance bar. Rather than working within a restricting zone of comfort, a concentrated effort is needed to rise above your present level of performance. Demand more of yourself. Push yourself to perform beyond the obvious minimal expectations.

What do you currently do well? How frequently are you doing it? Are you getting better at it? How can you get more out of yourself?

How deep are you diving within yourself to explore and experience new-found personal resources?

3. Position yourself for a deep dig. Psychologist Abraham Maslow determined that optimal mental health has seven requirements:

1) Take responsibility for your own feelings, including your own happiness.
2) Give up the luxury of blaming others for your shortcomings, disappointments, and suffering.
3) Face the consequences, even when the things you attempt and the risks you take bring about the worst possible results.
4) Seek to discover all the inner resources that are available to you, even though self-discovery is at times painful and demanding.
5) Act on your own feelings, rather than on the approval of others—even if this means conflict at times with those who are important to you.
6) Take responsibility for letting go of your own negativity, including letting yourself and other people off the hook.
7) Have compassion and empathy for yourself and for others, recognizing that having compassion is a very healing process.[6]

Maslow's mental health prerequisites set you up for optimal performance. They eliminate boundaries and excuses, putting you in the driver's seat to capitalize on possibilities.

No matter how you define success, regardless of how proud you are of your achievement, you've only discovered a tiny portion of all you are capable of doing. You've barely scratched the surface and owe it to yourself to dig a little deeper. You certainly need not settle for the way things are. There is more in you than what you've already accomplished.

Look for, plan, expect, and act to create a breakthrough experience. "Knowing is not enough, we must apply. Willing is not enough, we must do," wrote the German philosopher Goethe.[7] Far too few people act on their dreams, goals and ambitions and therefore, restrict ongoing success. The more you activate the digging devices, the more results you'll discover.

> He who would learn to fly one day must first learn to stand and walk and run and climb and dance; one cannot fly into flying.
> Friedrich W. Nietzsche[8]

Chapter 20

RETHINK WHAT YOU THINK

What you think means more than anything else in your life. More than what you earn, more than where you live, more than your social position, and more than what anyone else may think about you.

George Matthew Adams[1]

ROBERT COLLIER OFFERED THIS COMPACT look at thoughts: "We can do only what we think we can do. We can be only what we think we can be. We can have only what we think we can have. What we do, what we are, what we have all depend upon what we think."[2]

What have you been thinking about recently? During those times when you are not engaged in specific activity, what thoughts tend to dominate your mind? Your life is substantially molded by your thoughts. Heredity and environment provide a framework within which we build our thoughts. But, we choose how we mentally respond and what fills our mind minute by minute, day by day.

Your thoughts lead to attitudes which become beliefs (or values) which are seen in your behaviors and your behaviors ultimately become habits or a lifestyle. The present quality of your life is in direct proportion to your thoughts...what you dwell on and how you interpret your life's events.

Do you dwell on what's wrong, or what's right? Are you someone who is always against something, but rarely for anything? Do you see what is missing, or what is present? Are your eyes focused on what is beautiful, or do you tend to see a few dead blades of grass in a beautiful lush lawn? Are your thoughts constructive or destructive, uplifting, or discouraging? Do you tend to dwell on what you have, or what you lack, what cannot be done, or what is achievable? You see, if you wish your life could be different, if you dislike your daily grind, if you wish people would be more in tune to what you want, begin with you. Controlling what you allow your mind to dwell on today will alter your perspective of current events.

"Life does not consist mainly, or even largely, of facts and happenings," suggested Mark Twain. "It consists mainly of the storm of thoughts that are forever blowing through one's mind."[3] Never underestimate the power of those thoughts blowing through your mind. Life is full of natural laws and infallible principles. People succeed in life to the degree they understand the law of mental attraction. It states that you will draw to yourself that which you consistently think about. So, we are not necessarily what we think but what we think we are.

If you are lamenting today that your life is dull and repetitive or filled with problems and an undesirable future, remember this: almost everything that you experience in your life has been, or will be, created by your own thinking.

> There is a technique, a knack, for thinking, just as there is for doing other things. You are not wholly at the mercy of your thoughts, any more than they are you. They are a machine you can learn to operate.
>
> Alfred North Whitehead[4]

ATTITUDE: THE ANCHOR OF ATTITUDE

Chapter 21

MAKE EVERY HOUR A HAPPY HOUR

Real optimism is aware of problems but recognizes the solutions, knows about difficulties but believes they can be
overcome, sees the negatives but accentuates the positives,
is exposed to the worst but expects the best, has reason to
complain but chooses to smile.

William Arthur Ward[1]

HAVE YOU EVER BEEN AROUND people who are members of
the Ain't-Life-Awful club? They are such a joy to associate
with. Their conversations consist of complaining about
what a cruel world we live in, gossiping about the inadequacies of
others, voicing how unappreciated they feel and sharing how the
circumstances in their life are unfair. Club members are even know
to leave work at the end of the day and gather for "happy hour" from
5–7 p.m. to discuss how unhappy they are.

There is only one thing worse than being around people like
this—it's being one of those people.

"Attitude is the first quality that marks the successful man,"
Lowell Peacock suggested. "If he has a positive attitude and is a

positive thinker who likes challenges and difficult situations, then he has half his success achieved."[2] Your attitude, the way you see your world, determines the way you live, and your actions determine your accomplishment. Who you are today is a result of your attitude.

In his book, *The Winning Attitude,* author and speaker John C. Maxwell says that attitude...

- Is the "advance man" of our true selves.
- Has inward roots but outward fruits
- Is our best friend or our worst enemy
- Is more honest and more consistent than our words
- Is an outward look based on past experiences
- Is a thing which draws people to us or repels them
- Is never content until it is expressed
- Is the librarian of our past
- Is the speaker of our present
- Is the prophet of our future[3]

Attitude may not be the only variable that determines your level of success, but it is certainly a primary contributor. One of the most significant attitudinal factors affecting your life is your expectation of life. Norman Vincent Peale preached, "The person who sends out positive thoughts activates the world around him positively and draws back to himself positive results."[4]

You can learn to be more positive. There is no need to be saddled with the disheartening, deflating habit of seeing the dark side of life. If you're interested in creating an ongoing "happy hour," be assured there is only one person who can make it happen.

Begin by blocking out negativity. Stop yourself when you begin moaning, groaning, or complaining. Condition yourself to always search for the bright side of every situation. Run like crazy from negative, energy-draining people. Befriend co-workers who encourage others and display a spirit of gratitude. Focus on the present. Let go of past failures. Calm your anxiety about the future by expecting the best of today.

Be patient with yourself. Lifestyle changes take time, but the result is worth the effort and wait.

> The winner's edge is not in a gifted birth, a high IQ, or a talent. The winner's edge is all in the attitude, not aptitude. Attitude is the criterion for success.
>
> Denis Waitley[5]

Chapter 22

DO WHAT YOU LOVE AND SUCCESS WILL FOLLOW

The talent of success is nothing more than doing what you can do well; and doing well whatever you do, without the thought of fame.

Henry Wadsworth Longfellow[1]

A FUNDAMENTAL CHARACTERISTIC OF SUCCESSFUL PEOPLE is their ability to find out what they are good at and do it with a passion regardless of whether or not anyone notices. Curtis Carlson advises, "You must listen to your own heart. You can't be successful if you aren't happy with what you're doing."[2] The key here is being involved in something that utilizes your God-given abilities. I can think of nothing worse than attempting to motivate myself in a position or activity that does not compliment my talents.

Michael Korda said, "Your chances of success are directly proportional to the degree of pleasure you derive from what you do. If you are in a job you hate, face the fact squarely and get out."[3] As the old saying goes, "if the horse is dead, dismount." I don't think it's possible to ascend beyond where you are without first making sure that where you are is not where you want to be.

Before jumping overboard, consider this; if you have a job that fails to stimulate, fulfill, and energize you, maybe there is a simple solution. How about changing your attitude about your job? Maybe you don't have to dismount. Could it be possible that changing how you view your life could ignite a new flame?

Whit Hobbs wrote,

> Success is waking up in the morning, whoever you are, wherever you are, however old or young, and bounding out of bed because there's something out there that you love to do, that you believe in, that you're good at—something that's bigger than you are, and you can hardly wait to get at it again today.[4]

Approaching everything you do with that upbeat attitude is bound to result in success.

> Career is too pompous a word. It was a job, and I have always felt privileged to be paid for what I am doing.
>
> Barbara Stanwyck[5]

Chapter 23

CAREER-BUILDING PRINCIPLES

You pay a price for getting stronger.
You pay a price for getting faster.
You pay a price for jumping higher.
(But also) you pay a price for staying just the same.

H. Jackson Brown Jr.[1]

I F YOU WERE TO LEAVE your job today, what legacy would you leave? St. Augustine once said that adulthood begins when a person asks himself the question, "What do I want to be remembered for?"[2] Have you begun your adulthood? Do you have any idea what impact you are making on those around you? Are there certain character traits, actions or idiosyncrasies that will immediately make people think of you?

An unknown writer once communicated, "Methods are many; principles are few. Methods always change; principles never do."[3] Principles are heart issues. They are frequently an outgrowth of the attitudes we firmly hold. It's difficult to communicate in written word the emotion that ignites these motivating forces. Nevertheless, here are the unchangeable principles that have guided, formed, and directed my career.

1. My attitude about life will determine my quality of life.

Circumstances rarely dictate performance, but my perception of those events has dramatically impacted my ability to deal with them. I figure there are two ways of approaching life. Either alter the circumstances, or alter yourself to meet them. What really matters is not the way things are, but the way you think things are and how you decide to respond.

Your perception of and reaction to life's events will determine the impact they have on you. Every incident is merely an event waiting for you to develop an opinion about it. The attitude I display in life is a reflection of my internal beliefs, assumptions, and values. "You and I do not see things as they are," says Herb Cohen. "We see things as we are."[4]

This is more than positive thinking. It is a process of making a conscious decision about what you will dwell on and how you will interpret any given situation. It's a matter of perception, which is the result of mental habits.

2. There is a minuscule difference between success and failure. Success begins on the inside. NBA legend Michael Jordan said, "Heart is what separates the good from the great."[5]

The late Billy Martin was a controversial manager for the New York Yankees and established nonnegotiable standards for his players to follow. He let players know in no uncertain terms, "If you play for me, you play the game like you play life. You play it to be successful, you play it with dignity, you play it with pride, you play it aggressively and you play it as well as you possibly can."[6]

Are you getting the picture here? Successful people do a little more, raise the performance bar a little higher, expect higher results, and stick it out when things aren't going exactly as planned. Frank Lloyd Wright put it this way: "I know the price of success— dedication, hard work and an unremitting devotion to the things you want to see happen."[7]

Successful people continually monitor their attitude and make sure their energies are directed to their top priorities. They understand the need for total commitment to the tasks at hand and are determined to see it through to successful completion. Successful people are involved in a lifelong process of skill and competency development. They're not afraid to stand out from the crowd. In fact, they rather enjoy it.

Successful people do what's expected...and more. After Dallas won the Super Bowl in 1993, coach Jimmy Johnson commented, "I played for a national championship team, I coached a national championship team, and I coached a Super Bowl team. There's a common thread in all three: quality people who are committed to do their best."[8] It's the minuscule difference between success and failure.

3. Personal growth precedes personal fulfillment. Bruce Springsteen believes, "A time comes when you need to stop waiting for the man you want to become and start being the man you want to be."[9] You will never become what you ought to be until you begin doing what you ought to be doing to become what you want to be. Feeling good about your life is preceded by a willingness to learn, grow, and produce beyond your current accomplishments.

Sad is the day when a person becomes content with her life, what she thinks, and the results she is producing. A multitude of opportunities await us every day to expand. Failure to pursue those windows of possibility will leave us unfulfilled and dissatisfied with life. It's not life's fault.

"If you're not doing something with your life," began a Peace Corps commercial, "it doesn't matter how long it is."[10] When you stop growing and stretching, life becomes boring. You become boring. That's why it is so important to continually seek out challenges, people, new adventures, and learning situations that will stimulate incremental steps of continuous improvement. Unless you're in a growth mode, you're destined for mediocrity.

4. When I help others to be successful, I will be successful.
The most successful people in the world are those who help other people achieve more than they ever thought they could. Alan Lay McGinnis put it this way: "There is no more noble occupation in the world than to assist another human being—to help someone succeed."[11]

I'm often asked what I mean by, "helping someone succeed." Accept people with all of their irritating habits and idiosyncrasies—you have them, too. Always expect and discover the best in people. Listen without judgment and look them in the eye when they are talking. Pray for people. Share your affection. Laugh with people and cry with them as well. Send notes of encouragement and appreciation. Refrain from jealousy and anger. Celebrate people's successes with them. Go out of your way to be kind. Eliminate all ill will. Learn what is important to people and stand side by side with them in achieving their goals. Be a stimulant. Get excited about other people's lives, and make it a point to help every person you work, live, or socialize with to feel important.

Joann C. Jones, writing in *Guideposts*, relayed the following story:

> During my second year of nursing school our professor gave us a pop quiz. I breezed through the questions until I read the last one: "What is the first name of the woman who cleans the school?"
>
> Surely this was some kind of joke. I had seen the cleaning woman several times, but how would I know her name? I handed in my paper, leaving the last question blank.
>
> Before the class ended, one student asked if the last question would count toward the grade. "Absolutely," the professor said. "In your careers you will meet many people. All are significant. They deserve your attention and care, even if all you do is smile and say hello."
>
> "I've never forgotten that lesson. I also learned her name was Dorothy."[12]

From simply knowing their name, to walking step by step, side by side toward their dreams, your life will be filled with a multitude of moments to make a difference.

5. Walk the talk. St. Francis of Assisi once wisely said: "Preach the gospel at all times. If necessary, use words."[13] We get so busy in the activities of life, we forget above all else, what our life is communicating to others. Personality, work ethic, achievements, and our interactions with people display our good intentions. Who we are is the message. "So live that you wouldn't be ashamed to sell the family parrot to the town gossip," advised Will Rogers.[14]

In his book with Ken Blanchard, *Everyone's a Coach*, Don Shula tells of losing his temper near an open microphone during a televised game with the Los Angeles Rams. Millions of viewers expressed surprise and shock by Shula's profanity. Letters arrived from all over the country, voicing their dissatisfaction and disbelief that this man of integrity could display such behavior.

Shula could have been tempted to offer excuses, but he didn't. Everyone who included a return address received a personal apology. He closed each letter by stating, "I value your respect and will do my best to earn it again."[15]

Walking the talk doesn't mean living without mistakes but it does mean you are accountable for your behavior. Zig Ziglar was right. "Integrity," he says, "demands that you do the right thing so that you have fewer things to apologize for, explain away, or regret. Instead, cut your losses as quickly as possible after making a poor decision."[16] Be quick to apologize when you fail to live up to the standards you hold yourself accountable for.

Mark Twain knew how difficult it was to live an exemplary life. He once observed: "To do right is wonderful. To teach others to do right is even more wonderful—and much easier."[17]

6. Take responsibility for your life. Never allow someone or something outside of your control to prevent you from succeeding. Give up all excuses, the blame game, and finger pointing. "Success on any major scale requires you to accept responsibility," advises

Michael Korda, editor-in-chief of Simon & Schuster. "In the final analysis, the one quality that all successful people have is the ability to take on responsibility."[18]

You are completely responsible for what you do. Bern Williams has identified our modern day unwillingness to take responsibility by speculating, "If Adam and Eve were alive today, they would probably sue the snake."[19] We might chuckle at his suggestion, but I fear it is closer to the truth than most of us care to admit.

If you don't accept responsibility, you will soon identify yourself as a victim, and victims lead lives full of frustration, rationalization, blame, defensiveness, and excuses. Take responsibility for where you are and where you're going. You are accountable for the results. You always have been and always will be. That's probably why Ed Cole suggested: "Maturity doesn't come with age; it comes with acceptance of responsibility."[20]

7. Be willing to pay the price. I've observed two kinds of people: those who get things done and those who wait for all the conditions to be just right before attempting anything. There are those who do whatever it takes and those who continually protest, "That's not my job." Zig Ziglar recommends, "If you do the things you ought to do when you ought to do them, the day will come when you can do the things you want to do when you want to do them."[21]

Achievement is the result of doing what needs to be done, whether or not you feel like doing them. Don't wait to feel good before doing good. Pay the price now and experience the satisfaction of defying those little voices that tell you you're just not up to the task right now. "To achieve success, whatever the job we have, we must pay a price for success," said Vince Lombardi. "You have to pay the price to win and you have to pay the price to get to the point where success is possible. Most important, you must pay the price to stay there."[22]

When you pay the price day in and day out, no matter how tedious or demanding it might seem, you will be rewarded with a champion's lifestyle.

8. Live to give. "The measure of a life, after all, is not its duration but its donation," said Corrie Ten Boom.[23] Generosity is a marvelous quality.

In our society, money tends to be the measuring stick for giving. How big was his bonus? What was the increase in the bottom line? Our culture is obsessed with what people get.

Living to give involves so much more. The grave of Christopher Chapman in Westminster Abbey, bearing the date 1680, reads: *What I gave, I have; What I spent, I had; What I left, I lost; By not giving it.*[24]

It's difficult to convince selfish people to begin giving of their resources, time, and talent. Sometimes it's easiest to write a check and hope nothing more is required. Step out by sharing thoughtfulness, sensitivity, and kindness with those needing a bit of compassion. Never turn your head on a co-worker needing to feel included.

Help someone who cannot help you in return. Encourage those who cannot help themselves. Nurture someone in moving toward his potential. Create a generous heart, and heaven will be filled with people cheering when you get there.

9. Live every day to the fullest. "If you let yourself be absorbed completely," suggested Anne Morrow Lindbergh, "if you surrender completely to the moments as they pass, you live more richly in those moments."[25]

This is such a simple principle for living, I am almost embarrassed to include it in the list. Yet, it seems people are always preparing to live. Someday they'll enjoy their job. Someday they'll have time for those they love. Someday they'll get actively involved in the adventure of living. What are they waiting for? Someday may never come.

Life isn't a dress rehearsal for the main event. You are living the main event. Decide you will meet this week's assignments with a renewed passion. Capture the miracle of life by living every minute of every day to the fullest. Who knows, it might be your last.

10. Keep success in perspective. Singer Jon Bon Jovi's parents told him he could achieve anything, so he worked tirelessly on his musical career from the time he was sixteen. His band became phenomenally successful, but Jon Bon Jovi hit the wall and realized there had to be more to life than the continual pressure to produce another number one album or single. His wife, Dorothea, gave him the room and encouragement to put it all in perspective.

> "Today," says Bon Jovi, "I try to spend as much time on my marriage and parenting as I do on my career. For years we had a funny adage in our house that was, 'It's about me, me, me, the singer.' Now it's no longer about me, it's about them. We stay home, making sure the kids have a healthy, loving environment."[26]

Success is all about recognizing and appreciating the love and respect of those closest to you. What good is success if the people around you are being hurt in the process? What good is success if it is not contributing to the long-term health and benefit of those you love? What good is success if you don't have someone you love to share it with?

As much as I enjoy the pursuit of dreams, goals, and accomplishments, the long-term value is small compared to the privilege of savoring each day with those I love and respect.

That's it. The ten principles that guide my life are simple, but they've been effective in providing a compass for my personal and professional pursuits. How about you? Have you decided what unwavering, unchangeable principles will direct your life?

> Seize the moment. Remember all those women on the Titanic who waved off the dessert cart.
>
> Erma Bombeck[27]

Chapter 24

KNOW WHAT YOU VALUE
AND LIVE IT

I believe that a person ought to know what he believes, why he believes it and then believe it.

Charlie "Tremendous" Jones[1]

THE MIGHTY AND MAJESTIC QUEEN Mary was the largest ship to cross the oceans when it was launched in 1936. She enjoyed a distinguished career through four decades and a world war. Once retired, the Queen Mary was anchored in Long Beach, California, and converted into a hotel and museum. Restoration crews removed three massive smoke stacks slated to be scraped and painted. However, once detached from their supported location, the smoke stacks crumbled. All that remained of the 3/4-inch steel plate from which they had been constructed were several layers of paint that had been applied over the years. The steel had disintegrated.[2]

The Queen Mary suffered a condition common to humankind. Polished and attractive exteriors crumble over time if not supported by internal substance. Our lives and organizations break down, get out of balance, deteriorate, or even collapse without a solid set of values.

Our thinking produces attitudes resulting in values which are reflected in our personality. They serve as guidelines for how we behave and see the world. We speak our values through our possessions, personal appearance, gestures, and facial expressions. Our actions and the words we use are primary indicators of the values we possess.

Defining your values is not just a nice academic exercise. Rather, it is a fundamental step toward realizing fulfillment in life, satisfaction in career and authenticity in lifestyle. Carl Rogers said, "Clarifying your values is the essential first step toward a richer, fuller, more productive life."[3] To become and remain people who fully live life, we need to establish a foundation of unwavering values and beliefs.

Values simply identify what we cherish most in life. Values will ultimately help us determine if our pursuits are worth while.

To clarify your values, ask yourself:

- What do I believe in?
- In what guiding principles can I become constructively obsessed?
- What governs my life?
- What do I stand for?
- What puts meaning into my life?
- What qualities are important for my life to be complete?

This is not a simple exercise. Grappling for the right words is normal. Values are not contrived on the spur of the moment, given to negotiable or vacillating principles that come and go with each passing day. Rather, they are ingrained in the fiber of a person's heart and soul. As Joe Batten says, "Our value is the sum of our values."[4] It is impossible to separate personal value from personally held values.

Take the time to determine exactly what values are important to you. Your personal convictions, not those of others, will determine how you live. Whatever your list of value words, make them a living testament. Transform those words into guiding principles for everything you do. Values represent the uncompromised, essential, and enduring convictions people and organizations aspire to attain.

You will have many ups and downs and foggy times in your life. The starting point of high level, clear living is to think through and remain faithful to your values. As former President Jimmy Carter stated in his inaugural address, quoting one of his high school teachers: "We must adjust to changing times and still hold to unchanging principles."[5]

There is power in people who live their lives to the fullest when values and actions are congruent.

> Great successes are almost always people with a clear sense about what really matters ... a fundamental moral grounding, a sense of who they are and why they do what they do.
>
> Anthony Robbins[6]

Section Seven

IMPROVEMENT: BUILD A BETTER YOU

Chapter 25

PAY ATTENTION TO WHO YOU ARE

Character is what we do when no one is looking. It is not the same as reputation... success...achievement. Character is not what we have done, but who we are.

Bill Hybels[1]

C HARACTER HAS TO DO WITH how people are put together. It's the interaction between what they believe and what they do. Although talent is important to be successful in your job, character is imperative. Robert A. Cook was right, "There is no substitute for character. You can buy brains, but you cannot buy character."[2]

Career success is grounded in behavior that is consistent with the values we espouse. Violating personal values is harmful to the person, as well as the organization. Pretending leads to personal sabotage and self-protective behaviors. I agree with John Morley, who observed, "No man can climb out beyond the limitations of his own character."[3] When your character is strong, people trust you to perform up to your potential. When character is questionable, people never know what to expect.

Be a professional who knows what's right and does it even if it means putting forth substantially more effort. Doing what's easy or convenient isn't necessarily consistent with what's right.

Let your commitment to values drive your actions. Is it risk free? Will it be well received? Am I in the mood to do it? These are not the questions values-driven people ask. Are my behaviors in line with my ethical commitment? Do I believe in what I'm doing? Am I maintaining my integrity with this decision? These are the questions that surface when character is in charge.

Maintain the highest standards. Your character comes to life through your values, integrity and honesty...the consistency between your words and actions. Understand that your convictions might not initially win a popularity contest, especially if they violate "the way we've always done it." Remind yourself that the right things are not always rewarded and not everybody will be on your side.

Take full responsibility for your character. "Everybody's doing it" is juvenile and doesn't cut it. You can't put someone else in charge of your ethics. Try it, and you'll soon find yourself lowering your standards. "I'm just doing what I'm told" is a cop out. Character is a personal decision and quest. Your beliefs might coincide with the people you work with but ultimately character is an individual exercise.

Character driven people are willing to do the things emotion driven people will not do. They take pride in their dependability, commitment to excellence, willingness to serve others, solution minded approach to problems, and their internal drive...regardless of how they "feel." This isn't a sometime thing, or a 90 percent thing; either you have it, or you don't. Even brief leaks can be devastating.

Pay attention to who you are. It's more than a reputation. Reputation is what you are supposed to be. Character is what you are. Be encouraged by the words of Bobby Richardson who said, "Any man will command respect if he takes a stand and backs it up with his life."[4]

Hard work spotlights the character of people: some turn up their sleeves, some turn up their noses, and some don't turn up at all.

Sam Ewing[5]

Chapter 26

GETTING A BETTER
VIEW OF YOURSELF

Doubt yourself, and you doubt everything you see. Judge yourself and you see judges everywhere. But if you listen to the
sound of your own voice, you can rise above doubt and judgment, and you can see forever.

Nancy Kerrigan[1]

FROM *SUNDAY SERMONS* COMES THE story of a man who
brought his boss home for dinner for the first time. The boss
was very blustery, arrogant, and dominating! The little boy
in the family stared at his father's boss for most of the evening, but
did not say anything. Finally, the boss asked the little boy, "Why do
you keep looking at me like that, Sonny?" The little boy answered,
"My daddy says you are a self-made man." The boss beamed and
proudly admitted that indeed he was a self-made man. The little boy
said, "Well, if you are a self-made man, why did you make yourself
like that?"[2]

This little story prompts a chuckle every time I think about it. The little boy's comment also creates a few sobering thoughts. We all have our own struggles with becoming the persons we want to be. There may be times we even ask ourselves, "Why did I make myself like this?"

During one of my seminars, I often ask the question, "How many of you believe in yourself 100 percent?" Rarely does a hand go up. As I work my way down the percentage scale, somewhere between 50 and 75 percent, the majority of hands are raised. Two important questions are then posed to the group:

1) What keeps you from achieving 100 percent?
2) What would your work place be like if everyone believed in themselves 100 percent?

Believing in yourself 100 percent does not equate with arrogance, pride, or conceit. It's the maximum utilization of the gifts, abilities, and talents you've been given. On the flip side, believing in yourself half-way will not provide the motivation necessary to go beyond where you are.

Much of our insecurity about ourselves on the job is prompted by feeling we're not as good as other people and there's little chance things are going to get any better. To break out of this thinking, we need to reform our current beliefs and begin questioning the assumptions we make about ourselves.

Breaking through cemented images we have of ourselves is no easy task. Begin by seeing the person you want to become and then work backwards to make that image a reality. My friend Joe Batten says, "When we know who and what we wish to be, we will find it relatively easy to know what to do."[3] Begin acting like the person you want to become. Portray the confidence that person will have. Behave as if you are already that person. As you begin getting a better view of yourself, keep a few things in mind.

Be yourself. Brian Tracy believes, "The world will largely accept you at your own estimation. It is yourself that you have to convince before you can convince anyone else."[4]

Theologian Charles Spurgeon warned, "Beware of no one more than yourself; we carry our worst enemies within us."[5] It's important to discover who you really are—your character, values, and heart—before you attempt to build on what you have. Human being does indeed precede human doing.

Be genuine. Unfortunately, Ava Garder represented a lot of people when she said, "Deep down, I'm pretty superficial."[6]

Norman Vincent Peale once said, "It is a fact that you project what you are."[7] Be genuine. Phonies ultimately end up disliking themselves.

Be assured you are somebody special. Denis Waitley suggests, "Faith in yourself begins with understanding that God is always with you and within you."[8] Waitley's comment is comforting. God is bigger than any limitation you possess and capable of turning your greatest weakness into a strength.

There is a story told by Entertainer Roger Williams that has some relevance here. It seems the famous singer was on tour and stopped by a nursing home to visit his mother. He said he got lost looking for her room and was wandering around somewhat confused when an elderly woman came up to him and looked at him with an intensely curious, but recognizing stare. After a moment, he awkwardly broke the silence asking, "Do you know who I am?"

Surveying him from head to toes, she replied, "No, but if you go to the front desk, they can tell you."[9]

We don't need someone else telling us who we are, but to increase our value to the company, our co-workers and customers, knowing who we are and striving to be what we want to become is important. Zig Ziglar reminds us: "You cannot consistently perform in a manner which is inconsistent with the way you see yourself."[10] Therefore, staying neutral is not an option. We need move forward to discipline ourselves toward positive, constructive action that moves us continually in the direction of becoming all we can be.

That's how you get a better view of yourself.

> You are free to choose where you work, what you do, and with whom you will work. But who and what you become is hanging in the balance. Before you take a job or position, remind yourself that what will go on in the workplace will change you, and ask yourself whether or not the change will be in harmony with your mission statement.
>
> Tony Campolo[11]

Chapter 27

BE THE BEST YOU CAN BE

If you want to achieve excellence, you can get there today. As of this second, quit doing less than excellent work.

Thomas Watson[1]

JOHN C. MAXWELL, WRITING IN *Developing the Leader Within You,* says "Most people have a desire to look at the exception instead of the desire to become the exceptional."[2] Why? It takes a ton of effort to become exceptional and very little effort to find excuses for why we aren't performing at our best. There is a personal price to pay to excel in your career. No shortcuts are available.

"Excellence," says Pat Riley, "is the gradual result of always striving to do better."[3] Notice Riley didn't say, "If you do this one thing, you'll have mastered the formula for excellence." Reaching your optimum performance requires small steps to help you grow so you're prepared for your next level of performance.

Different things seem to work for different people. However, a few of the strategies are relatively universal. Consider the following approaches for planning your excursion away from average toward your peak performance.

1. Fix The Flaws. Running back Rashaan Salaam's outstanding rushing career in college earned him the Heisman Trophy in 1995. He was drafted by the Chicago Bears, and although he led the bears in rushing during the rookie season, opponents spotted a weakness in his game. Salaam was prone to fumble. In fact, he gave up the ball nine times.

According to the *Chicago Tribune*, the Chicago Bears' coaching staff devised a practical drill to correct the problem. They tied a long strap around a football. As Rashaan ran with the ball tightly clutched against his body, another player ran behind him yanking on the strap. Rashaan learned to squeeze the ball with such power that it could not be forced free.[4]

People who are committed to excellence in their careers identify what top notch performance would look like and then move towards that standard. As this process evolves, needed corrections unfold and adjustments are made to ensure a steady progress toward the ideal. Minor flaws, imperfections, and less than desirable outcomes are bound to surface. That's a natural part of the process. What separates the excellent from the mediocre performers is the determination to correct faults that undermine their desire to be the best they can be. As Oliver Cromwell said in the early 17th century, "The person who stops being better, stops being good."[5] It's a never ending quest.

I'm not an advocate for investing massive attention and energy on fixing what's wrong and letting the strengths take care of themselves. Quite the contrary. Yet, you can't overlook those issues that keep you from scaling new heights, refining your expertise or achieving expanded results. But just because you remove or correct the weaknesses doesn't mean everything will be perfect. You might have an error free day, but not necessarily one that could be defined as excellent. Rashaan Salaam may not fumble the ball during an entire game, but that doesn't mean he has a successful day in the backfield. More is needed than "just" managing our limitations or weaknesses.

2. Find Your Sweet Spot. After decades of work as a consultant with major companies and a prolific writing career, Peter Drucker made this observation:

> The great mystery isn't that people do things badly but that they occasionally do a few things well. The only thing that is universal is incompetence. However, nobody ever commented, for example, that the great violinist, Jascha Heifetz, probably couldn't play the trumpet very well.[6]

Finding that niche, talent, or interest where excellence can be achieved is a great way to maximize your efforts. When we find that "sweet spot," as in tennis or golf, increased power and control are at our disposal.

Find your sweet spot and become the best you can be. Take a common thing and do it uncommonly well. As Alfred North Whitehead put it, "Doing little things well is the way toward doing big things better."[7]

Capitalizing on your sweet spot keeps you reaching, stretching to perfect your skills and to outdo yesterday. You may see slow improvement, but it's enough to eventually add up to a significant increase in your expertise. Use your sweet spots to trigger dramatic performance breakthroughs, protect your career, improve your value to the company, and prepare the way for a bright future. Think of it as a daily pursuit of perfection that will upgrade your contribution to the team and organization.

3. Focus On Doing Your Best. In an effort to keep up in this fast-paced world, some people lower their standards and expect less than excellence. Sacrifices are made in the name of efficiency. Such a move can reduce a person's performance to mediocrity.

With tremendous pressure coming from every direction for you to increase productivity and shorten the time to do it, it's easy to fall into doing what's "good enough." It appears to be the quickest way to satisfy everybody. Unfortunately, mediocrity will catch up with you. You'll become dissatisfied with your own results, customers begin to drift away, supervisors notice that you're beginning to get lax, and the organization's reputation slips.

Orison Swett Marden reminded us that, "There is no excuse for incompetence in this age of opportunity; no excuse for being second-class when it is possible to be first-class, and when first-class is in demand everywhere."[8]

Are you doing your best? Raise your standards. Establish a baseline you can be proud of. Make no exceptions. Instead of accepting less than your best, improve upon your personal best. "Aim at perfection in everything," suggested Lord Chesterfield, "though in most things, it is unattainable. However, they who aim at it, and persevere, will come much nearer to it than those whose laziness and despondency make them give it up as unattainable."[9]

Reach for new heights. Go above and beyond the call of duty. Do more than others expect. Never accept so-so performance in yourself or those around you.

> Over and over again mediocrity is promoted because real worth isn't to be found.
>
> Kathleen Norris[10]

Chapter 28

JUMP IN...YOU'LL GET USED TO IT!

Life is like a taxi. The meter just keeps a-ticking whether you
are getting somewhere or just standing still.

Lou Erickson[1]

THE LAKE WHERE OUR FAMILY frequently vacations warms up to comfortable swimming temperatures around the end of June. I've made it a tradition for many years to take my first dip in early May. Call me crazy, but traditions are hard to break.

This year I hesitated on the dock. The memories of frigid temperatures, burning skin and frozen toes made me wonder whether this annual event should be called off in favor of more reasonable behavior.

Just as I almost convinced myself that warmer water temperatures would be more inviting, I heard the voice of my five-year-old nephew. "Just jump in, Uncle Glenn. "You'll get used to it!"

How could I resist? I jumped.

Life's like that. It's virtually impossible to ease your way in. Sometimes, you have to jump in with both feet and get used to the invigorating, shocking, enjoyable, successful, or disappointing experiences you encounter.

There are no quick fixes in life. No master plan has been designed to insure continual success. There are no easy roads to achievement. Life is a series of calculated actions deliberately taken to attain the results you desire.

Don't get caught in life waiting for someone to ring your doorbell and announce, "Have I got a life for you!" People are too busy designing their own lives. And, it's ludicrous to think we can sit in an easy chair hoping things start going our way. Dreams are fulfilled by taking action, not through endless thinking about doing something. Why go to all the bother of even thinking about accomplishments if you're not willing to jump in?

Face it, life is not a dress rehearsal. This is not a warm-up for the real thing. This is it. This is the big show, your debut. It's okay to scream, get sweaty palms, and feel anxious. A bit of uncertainty, fear, and helplessness are normal. Action works like a power-inducing drug to relieve those immobilizing feelings. When the shift lever is put in drive and the pedal is pushed to the middle, momentum will provide you the power necessary to keep on going.

> Life is always walking up to us and saying, "Come on in, the living's fine," and what do we do? Back off and take its picture.
> Russell Baker[2]

Section Eight

ACTION: MAKE THINGS HAPPEN

Chapter 29

COMPLETE UNCOMPLETED TASKS

Nothing is so fatiguing as the eternal hanging on of an uncompleted task.

William James[1]

WHAT DO YOU REMEMBER MOST—the tasks you have completed or those you have yet to do? Most people immediately respond: "I remember most the things I have left to do."

I'm always challenged (and often embarrassed) when I arrive home at night and my wife asks, "What did you do today?" There are some days I must honestly respond, "I don't know for sure. But it took me all day to do it."

Failure to make significant progress completing work demands is a major source of frustration, stress, and disappointment. Existing in a frantic whirlwind of commitments and activities is not the same as producing results. In fact, an estimated one-third of the American workforce doesn't accomplish what it sets out to do each day. Is it any wonder we have a nation of unfulfilled workers?

Henry David Thoreau observed: "It's not enough to be industrious, so are the ants. What are you industrious about?"[2]

What is your definition of work? Is it a series of activities and responsibilities? If so, then work is viewed as a verb. Everybody works, but not everybody is productive.

Productive people see work as what they are able to achieve. It is a noun. What evolves out of completed tasks is a feeling of being in control, increased productivity, heightened satisfaction, increased time for other responsibilities, and more energy to be creative. Until we develop a mindset that what we achieve is far more important than being busy, completing uncompleted tasks will not be a priority.

Review your pending assignments, the pile of unread journal articles, correspondence awaiting your reply, and the return phone calls you've been avoiding. Simplify your approach. Plan to unclutter your life (and desk) by seeing these responsibilities through to completion.

Completion produces a satisfaction that the result has been achieved. You can mark it off your to-do list and get a fresh start. There's a new freedom to pursue the next priority. Creativity increases. Your energy tank will be refilled and you will be able to refocus attention. A renewed momentum is in place.

Look for ways to bring closure and completion to your daily assignments. We live in a time when working hard is not nearly as important as getting work done. You will be recognized and remembered for what you have done, not for how busy you were or how good your intentions were.

Simple Hint: If you have difficulty bringing closure to your work, pretend you're going on vacation next week. I'm convinced a national survey would produce a phenomenal correlation between efficiency, effectiveness, results, and the timing of vacations.

What you accomplish in life depends almost completely upon what you make yourself do. Perfect concentration and a great desire will bring a person success in any field of work he chooses. The very first thing one should do is to train the mind to concentrate upon the essentials and discard the frivolous and unimportant. This will assure real accomplishment and ultimate success.

Lyndon Johnson[3]

Chapter 30

HALF FINISHED

If you are wearing out the seat of your pants before you do your shoe soles, you're making too many contacts in the wrong place.

Anonymous[1]

WINTER IN THE MIDWEST PROVIDES ample opportunity for any youngster with a little gumption to benefit from the lack of motivation displayed by others. After a heavy snowfall, we would grab our shovels and go in search of adults discouraged by nature's actions. Youthful ingenuity led us to people whose driveways were half finished. In fact, hearing someone say, "Can't you see I'm already half finished?" tickled our hearts. These people lost interest in their activity and would usually turn over their driveway (and their money) to our ambitions and willingness to finish what they had started.

Stick-to-itiveness is a quality lacking in the day-to-day affairs of many people. We can never be what we ought to be until we start doing what we ought to be doing. Then, we need to continue doing what we ought to be doing so we can achieve what we are capable of achieving. "You will never stub your toe standing still," reflected

Charles F. Kettering. "The faster you go, the more chance there is of stubbing your toe, but the more chance you have of getting somewhere."[2]

Don't get bogged down in preparing to take action. Preparation is often a stall tactic, an excuse for fearing what your actions might produce or fail to produce. Very little can be accomplished unless you go ahead and do it before you're ready. When you hear someone constantly talking about what they are going to do tomorrow, rest assured they probably said the same thing yesterday.

A lifestyle of inactivity, procrastination, or quitting perpetuates itself. There is a cure. William James, the father of American psychology, suggested three rules for making things happen in life:

1. Start immediately.
2. Do it flamboyantly.
3. No exceptions.[3]

Put another way, get up, get active, wear out your soles, and stick to it with unwavering tenacity. "To know what has to be done, and then do it," said Sir William Osler, "comprises the whole philosophy of practical life."[4]

> Take time to deliberate; but when the time for action arrives, stop thinking and go in.
>
> Andrew Jackson[5]

Chapter 31

Filling Holes or Planting Trees

If you ever think you're too small to be effective, you've never been in bed with a mosquito.

Anita Roddick[1]

ORGANIZATIONS NEED PEOPLE WHO WANT to make a difference, not those who simply keep busy. These "busy" people do busy work without productivity. These people are a dime a dozen.

On the other hand, co-workers who are excited about their responsibilities recognize the importance of their roles, apply themselves to the job at hand, and desire to improve the way things are, achieve appreciable results. No matter how seemingly unimportant or insignificant their role, they keep moving forward, positioning themselves to perform on a higher plane.

Organizations need people willing to take initiative by making bold moves to advance the organization's effectiveness. There's plenty of room for people who constantly think of new ways to contribute to the team. Shattering the status quo, endorsing risk, and making gutsy moves to benefit the organization isn't written in their job descriptions. These are the unwritten qualifications that separate mediocre and successful people. As William Arthur Ward said, "Blessed is the person who sees the need, recognizes the responsibility and actively becomes the answer."[2]

Watching people who lack this type of initiative is frustrating. As they sit around waiting for further instructions or permission to act, a countless number of growth opportunities pass them by. It's as if they are orchestrating the death of their career.

Business giant Conrad Hilton suggested, "Success seems to be connected with action. Successful people keep moving. They make mistakes, but they don't quit."[3] People who take audacious action may not always be right, but it's proof they are interested in doing more than staying busy—filling a hole. Besides, they normally keep on investing themselves until they get things right. They crush through old habits and move beyond the routine of doing the same things, the same way, every day.

We live in a fast-paced, impatient world that won't wait around for those who wait to be perfect before taking action. Focused energy, in the face of uncertainty, is rewarded.

Make yourself more valuable. Emphasize action. Don't get bogged down in purposeless activity. Seek radical achievement. There is always a hole to be filled. Don't wait for someone else to plant the tree. Take the initiative. Very little will be accomplished unless you go ahead and do it. Others will follow.

In the words of Theodore Roosevelt, "Get action. Do things; be sane, don't fitter away your time; create, act, take a place wherever you are and be somebody. Get action."[4]

> Four little words sum up what has lifted most successful individuals above the crowd: a little bit more. They did all that was expected of them and a little bit more.
>
> A. Lou Vickery[5]

Chapter 32

THERE ARE ONLY SO MANY TOMORROWS

Somebody should tell us right at the start of our lives that we are dying. Then we might live life to the limit, every minute of every day. Do it! I say. Whatever you want to do, do it now! There are only so many tomorrows.

Michael Landon[1]

WHAT IF SOMEONE ASKED ME to write on a index card how I lived my life to the fullest so that my advice could be passed on to other generations? What would my card say? I never finished the card but thought I would pass on a few thoughts that ran through my head.

Robin Williams as Professor Keating in *Dead Poet's Society* declares,

I stand up on my desk to remind myself that we must constantly look at things in a different way. You see, the world looks very different from up here. Just when you think you know something you have to look at it in another way. Even though it may seem silly or wrong, you must try. When you read, don't just consider what the author thinks; consider what you think. Boys, you must strive to find your own voice because the longer you wait to begin, the less likely you will find it at all. Thoreau said, "Most men lead lives of great desperation." Don't be resigned to that. Break out! Don't just walk off the edge like lemmings, look around you ... Dare to strike out and find new ground.[2]

I love that scene. Professor Keating challenges a group of sophisticated, uptight, adventure impoverished students to push their lives over the edge of ordinary existence.

Another scene in the movie shows Mr. Keating escorting the boys to the school's trophy case displays. Photos of earlier graduating classes are prominently displayed.

"Look at these pictures, boys," Keating challenges. "The young men you behold had the same fire in their eyes that you do. They planned to take the world by storm and make something magnificent of their lives. That was years ago. Now the majority of them are pushing up daisies. How many of them really lived out their dreams? Did they do what they set out to accomplish?"

Then, with a dramatic move, Keating leans into his astounded class and passionately whispers, "Carpe diem! Seize the day!"[3]

Contrast that attitude with the one depicted in the classic comedy movie "Groundhog Day" starring Bill Murray. In the movie, Murray repeatedly wakes up at the exact same time on the exact same day. Every day is the same "Groundhog Day," which he lives over and over again.[4] That script not only made for good humor, it also depicts the lifestyle of many people. They rise at the same time, eat the same thing for breakfast, head for work at the same time, slide into their comfortable work habits, punch out, and head for home. Then, they repeat the same thing again tomorrow.

It is relatively easy to physically live a long life in America. Statistics indicate 88,361 of every 100,000 persons reach 50 years of age, more than 70,000 make it to 70, and almost 17,000 live to age 85 or more. That doesn't mean these same numbers live lives of significance and value. We have little to do with how life begins and, in some cases, the length of it. But we can significantly affect the outcome.

Cultivating attitudes and skills, seizing the initiative to master each moment, dismantling beliefs that life must be fair and good at all times, and establishing priorities that reflect personal values are all attributes indicative of people investing fully in the process of living.

I read a powerful story about the late Jim Valvano, former North Carolina State basketball coach. At age forty-seven he was suffering from terminal spinal cancer and reflecting on his life. He recalled an incident as a twenty-three-year-old intensely competitive coach of a small college team. "Why is winning so important to you?" his players asked.

"Because the final score defines you," Valvano replied.

"No," the players insisted. "Participation is what really matters. Trying your best, regardless of whether you win or lose—that's what defines you."

Twenty-four years later, struggling with the horrible effects of chemotherapy, hanging onto life by a thread, Valvano realized, "Those kids were right. It's effort, not result. It's trying. God, what a great human being I could have been if I'd had this awareness back then."[5]

Life isn't intended to be an all-or-nothing fight between winning and losing, misery and bliss, boredom and excitement. Life isn't inherently good or bad. Life is life. Sometimes it's okay, sometimes it's invigorating. Sometimes comfortable. Sometimes unpleasant. Always inviting us to make the most of it.

You may need to discover new ways of seeing yourself, life, and the possibilities contained in both. The journey starts when you believe that your life can become renewed and the future impacted.

What a great human being you'll become when you endorse the principle that at the closing of each day you're content with the way you lived it. Seize the day!

What would your card say?

> Success is living up to your potential. That's all. Wake up with a smile and go after life ... Live it, enjoy it, taste it, smell it, feel it.
>
> Joe Kapp[6]

DEVELOPMENT: SUCCESS IS WHERE YOU FIND IT

Chapter 33

Developing Your Picture of Success

Remember, when you can, that the definition of success has changed. It is not only survival, the having—it is the quality of every moment of your life, the being. Success is not a destination, a place you can ever get to; it is the quality of the journey.

Jennifer James[1]

THE TOPIC OF SUCCESS OFTEN produces two dominant questions: What is success? How do you attain it? My journey to answer these questions and understand success has taken a number of twists and turns. The older I get, the more reflective I become on the subject and the less dogmatic I am about my observations. I have concluded that everyone needs to determine for themselves what success will mean to them.

For me, that person is a success who enjoys life, lives it to the fullest, and helps others do the same. Success is ultimately an individual feeling of fulfillment, satisfaction, and a desire to continue growing. Dr. John Maxwell defined success in *The Success Journey* as, "Knowing my purpose in life, growing to maximum potential, and sowing seeds that benefit others." In your life long success journey, Dr. Maxwell suggests, "Two things are required for success: the right picture of success and the right principles for getting there."[2]

What is the right picture of success? Real estate magnet Donald Trump suggested, "The real measure of success is how happy you are. I have a lot of friends who don't have a lot of money, but they are a lot happier than I am, so therefore I say that they are probably more successful."[3] That's a nice thought, but there are countless people who are always searching for something more to make them happy. In fact, I'm convinced some people are only happy when they're unhappy. Happiness can certainly be one of many by-products of success, but rarely a measure of success.

Many other so-called success guideposts lead to equally miserable results. The attainment of the ideal job, achieving financial security, landing a major account, completing a challenging project, or building the dream home are empty measurements of success. That's not to say these aren't honorable pursuits, but when used as success indicators, they will fall far short of being classified as enduring factors.

When it comes to the principles of success, William Arthur Ward offered this recipe: "Study while others are sleeping, work while others are loafing, prepare while others are playing, and dream while others are wishing."[4] What a marvelous starting point!

According to a 1993 *Pryor Report*, executives from two hundred of the nation's largest companies were asked, "Of successful people you have met over the years, which of the following is the main reason for their success?"

- Contacts
- Determination
- Hard work
- Knowledge
- Luck

In response, 40 percent of these high-powered executives indicated success was due to hard work, 38 percent said determination, and 78 percent attributed success to hard work and determination.[5]

A combination of hard work and determination define Olympic gold medalist Janet Evans. As a seventeen-year-old high school senior, Evans took Seoul, Korea by storm in the Fall of 1988. This Olympic wonder didn't settle for just one medal, she won three: the 400-meter freestyle, the 800-meter freestyle and the 400-meter individual medley. If that isn't enough, Evans shattered her own world record with a 4:03.85, clocking in the 400-meter freestyle.[6]

How was this young, untested Olympic swimmer able to excel under constant attention, pressure and media focus? For five years prior, beginning at age twelve, Evans committed herself to a rigorous daily training schedule. She began the day at 4:45 a.m. with a four-mile swim, followed by school, then homework and back to the pool for a 9,000 meter swim. Janet was home by 6 p.m. for supper, a bit more homework, and in bed by 8 p.m. to prepare her body for another demanding day. Hard work and determination enabled Janet Evans to become the winner of forty-five U.S. National Titles and the holder of six American records.

"But wait," you might say, "I thought success and achievement were not synonymous." When you combine knowing where you are going, striving to become your personal best, and helping others to do the same, with the qualities of hard work and unwavering dedication, good things happen. Janet Evans meshed together her picture of success and the required effort to attain it. "Success," suggests Brian Tracy, "comes when you do what you love to do, and commit to being the best in your field.."[7]

Violinist Isaac Stern believed,

> There should be at least three cardinal rules for success in personal achievement, whatever the field may be:
>
> - Complete passionate devotion to whatever field you have chosen

- The need to concentrate, to the exclusion of all else, when working on, thinking about, or executing whatever discipline you have chosen
- An utter pitiless sense of self-criticism, far greater than that which any outsider could give[8]

Brian Tracy believes, "If you have the desire to change, the decisiveness to take action, the determination to persist on your forward track, and the discipline to make yourself do whatever you need to do, your self-confidence and success are inevitable."[9]

Successful people understand that success is all about who you are, and what you are doing every moment of your life to cause good things to happen. Don't complicate the issue of success. Develop a clear picture of what success will mean to you and then endeavor to do something every day that will make that picture a reality.

> A Thoroughbred horse never looks at the other horses. It just concentrates on running the fastest race it can.
>
> Henry Fonda[10]

Chapter 34

WHAT IMPRESSION WOULD YOU HAVE MADE?

You always do whatever you want to do. This is true of every act. You may say you had to do something, or that you were forced to, but actually, whatever you do, you do by choice. Only you have the power to choose for yourself. The choice is yours. You hold the tiller. You can alter the course you choose in the direction of where you want to be—today, tomorrow, or in a distant time to come.

W. Clement Stone[1]

I'VE STROLLED THROUGH AIRPORTS OBSERVING uptight and stressed travelers. "What do you mean you can't deliver?" I overheard a sales person scream into the phone. "How could the flight leave without me?" demanded a frustrated vacationer. Countless people shuffled, ran, or slowly meandered through the airport hallways with a scowl on their face and pain in their eyes.

Two men, sitting near me on one flight sounded like dueling banjos as they downgraded, bam blasted, and generally ripped apart their companies. According to them, they weren't being paid enough, worked too many hours, and their bosses didn't have the slightest idea how difficult their jobs were. "Why in the world are they still on board?" I thought to myself.

Leonard, on the other hand, either loved his job at an airport coffee stand or he was preparing to audition for a professional acting career. His entertaining comments, happy feet, and friendly demeanor prompted me to increase the tip I had intended to give. I revisited him on my return through the airport later in the week. He was still there. Same song... second verse.

Bill loved his job as well. He told me so on our trip from the hotel to the airport. "Never thought I could enjoy work this much," this sixty-something courtesy van driver told me. He was genuinely interested in what I did for a living, had strong, positive feelings about his employer and was well versed in the community and nation's current events. The fifteen minute ride went far too fast. Bill gave courtesy drivers a **great** name.

Audrey also impressed me. She worked at the front desk of the Bismarck, North Dakota, hotel where I was speaking. I had limited time after my seminar to get to the airport. I also needed to have the hotel UPS a box back to my office. Audrey immediately took charge, filled out the paperwork, weighed the box, smiled, and assured me she would personally take care of it. I extended my heartfelt thanks. "No problem," she responded, "that's what I'm here for." I like people like that!

Beau was equally impressive. He wore a seemingly permanently-affixed-massive-smile across his face that only slightly diminished as he hoisted my heavy luggage into the van. "Is there somewhere we can stop on the way to the airport for a cup of gourmet coffee," I asked. "You bet," he replied. He shared his passion for the theater and his aspirations to perform on stage. Beau had already experienced some acting success and was excited about his casting in an upcoming production of *Guys and Dolls*. I liked his spirit. He hadn't done anything special, except to make me feel good about my visit.

As we navigated the darkened skies on the final flight home, I watched a curly haired, blue-eyed, two-and-a-half year old across the aisle. This vibrant little thing hadn't yet realized it was night time. She sang. She laughed. She turned to hold her daddy's hand as her big eyes looked into his, "I love you, daddy!" Then, she commenced softly singing her A-B-C's song. Her mother smiled, nodding approval while struggling to stay awake.

Who will this little girl grow up to be? Will she become a rigid, uptight, stressed out, weary adult? Or, will she become another Leonardo, Audrey, Beau, or Bill? This sweet little thing has a multitude of choices to make as she grows up. These choices will determine who we see in twenty, thirty, or forty years. I only hope she looks to those who have made responsible choices as her models.

Imagine that you are the adult that little girl models her life after. What will the result be? Will she love her chosen career? Will she find ways to positively impact the lives of people she comes in contact with? Will she continue smiling and innocently enjoying the little blessings of life? Will she face life's challenges with gusto and anticipation?

I endorse William Jennings Bryant's belief that, "Destiny is not a matter of chance but a matter of choice. It is not a thing to be waited for. It is a thing to be achieved."[2] You can control your destiny and perspective of life, your job, and the people you encounter. The choices you make today, tomorrow, and next week build on each other to create a lifestyle that ultimately determines who you become, what you do, and what you have.

We can choose to welcome each new day with interest and curiosity, and as a new adventure, a new experience. We can also choose to dread every waking minute. We can choose to see an opportunity in every situation we encounter, or a crisis waiting to happen. We can choose to smile or scowl. We can choose to plant seeds of fear, doubt, and dislike or we can sow seeds of faith, hope, and love. We can choose to see others' positive characteristics and find them interesting and enjoyable, or we can choose to identify their annoyances and avoid interaction. The choice menu is endless.

I've learned you can give people a position or a job, but you cannot give them the qualities to be successful. People must choose whether or not to develop their qualities. Nothing will have a greater impact on your future than your decision to develop or bypass the characteristics of success. Rate yourself from one (low) to seven (high) on the commonly accepted qualities for job success:

	Low				High		
Enthusiasm	1	2	3	4	5	6	7
Understanding Others	1	2	3	4	5	6	7
Ambition	1	2	3	4	5	6	7
Knowledge of the Job	1	2	3	4	5	6	7
Creativity	1	2	3	4	5	6	7
Self-Motivation	1	2	3	4	5	6	7
Desire to Excel	1	2	3	4	5	6	7
Self-Discipline	1	2	3	4	5	6	7
Interest in the Job	1	2	3	4	5	6	7
Attitude	1	2	3	4	5	6	7
Decision Making	1	2	3	4	5	6	7
Commitment	1	2	3	4	5	6	7
Problem Solving	1	2	3	4	5	6	7

Admit to the poor choices you've made, leaving these qualities underdeveloped. You can decide to alter the course of your life, the satisfaction you experience in your career. You can make yourself become whatever you long to be, gain confidence and strip away the barriers limiting your potential.

You are who you are and where you are today because of the choices you've made. If you want things to change, you have to make better choices. If you want to be a model of happiness, fulfillment and contentment, eliminate the destructive choices that block these positive results. Act, walk, talk, and conduct yourself as the model person you can become. The only way you're going to make a change is to infuse yourself with a sense of urgency that continually nudges you to follow through.

Choose today to be the type of person that little girl on the airplane would be excited to become.

> The common idea that success spoils people by making them vain, egotistical, and self-complacent is erroneous; on the contrary, it makes them, for the most part, humble, tolerant, and kind. Failure makes people bitter and cruel.
>
> Somerset Maugham[3]

Chapter 35

THE MAKINGS OF SUCCESS

Success is like Haley's Comet, you know. Every now and then it just comes around.

Ross Perot[1]

S UCCESS MIGHT JUST COME AROUND, but most often it is the result of focused and concentrated effort. Reflecting upon her years of public service, Margaret Thatcher suggested that, "Success is having a flair for the things that you are doing. Knowing that is not enough; you have got to have hard work and a certain sense of purpose."[2]

Dr. Tom Morris, in his book *True Success*, offers these additional guidelines for achieving success:

1. A conception of what you want. This means a vision, goal or set of goals, "powerfully imagined."
2. A confidence to see it through. Without it, you'll never overcome obstacles.
3. A concentration on what it takes. Prepare and plan and do. "The world has more participants, more catalysts, agents of change..."

4. A consistency in what you do. Be stubborn and persistent—even after failure.
5. A commitment of emotional energy. Emerson said, "Nothing great was ever achieved without enthusiasm."
6. A character of high quality. Integrity inspires trust and gets people pulling for you.
7. A capacity to enjoy the process. The journey should be fun as well as challenging.[3]

As you can see, there are no new fangled success secrets. The principles and disciplines of success have been around since the beginning of time. The real issue here is that we cannot enjoy the benefits of success without the investment of sacrifice. Those people who want to wake up successful need to wake up. It's not going to happen that way. "Success, real success in any endeavor," says James Rouche, "demands more from an individual than most people are willing to offer—not more than they are capable of offering."[4] In other words, none of the writings, principles, secrets, processes work...unless you do.

I couldn't wait for success—so I went ahead without it.
Jonathan Winters[5]

FACE YOUR CHALLENGES HEAD ON

Obstacles are like wild animals. They are cowards but they will bluff you if they can. If they see you are afraid of them...they are liable to spring upon you; but...if you look them squarely in the eye, they will slink out of sight.

Orison Swett Marden[1]

T HERE HAVE BEEN TIMES I feel like Mother Teresa when she said, "I know God will not give me anything I can't handle. I just wish that he didn't trust me so much."[2]

It's a bit like the lion tamer who put this advertisement in the paper: "Lion tamer wants tamer lion."

The Biblical character Joseph probably felt the same way. If anyone ever faced obstacles, Joseph did. His brothers hated him. He was sold into slavery. He was falsely accused and thrown into an Egyptian prison. Yet he continued trusting the Lord and walking by faith. Rather than causing him to stumble, hardships were stepping stones to his success and his service for the Lord.

In *A View From the Zoo*, Gary Richmond provides an entertaining and educational description of the birth of a giraffe.

The first things to emerge are the baby giraffe's front hooves and head. A few minutes later the remaining body of the newborn is hurled forth, falls ten feet, and lands on its back. Within seconds, the baby giraffe rolls to an upright position with his legs tucked under his body. From this position, he experiences the world for the first time and shakes off the birthing fluid from his eyes and ears.

The mother giraffe lowers her head long enough to take a quick look at her new responsibility. Then she positions herself directly over her calf. She waits for a moment, and then she does the most unreasonable thing. She swings her long, powerful leg outward and kicks her baby, so that it is sent sprawling head over heals out of control. The newborn lies motionless.

When it doesn't get up, the process is repeated over and over again. The struggle to rise is thwarted by undeveloped limbs and muscles. As the baby calf grows tired, the mother kicks it again to stimulate its efforts... Finally, the calf struggles to stand for the first time on its wobbly legs.

Then the mother giraffe does the unspeakable. She kicks it off its feet again. Why? She wants her newborn to remember how it got up. In the wild, baby giraffes must be able to get up as quickly as possible to stay with the herd, where there is safety. Lions, hyenas, leopards, and wild hunting dogs all enjoy the pursuit of young giraffes, and they'd get it too, if the mother didn't teach her calf to get up quickly to escape.[3]

The birth of the giraffe is not unlike experiences we encounter in life. There are times when it seems we just stand up after one trial only to be knocked down again by the next. If only we could see how important it is to jump back up and recover from the unfair blow. Remaining motionless opens the door to being ambushed. Positioning ourselves in ready position prepares us to meet the next challenge with greater insight.

Difficult circumstances often result in a new perspective on life. People begin to see the world differently from before. They get a fresh perspective on their abilities, blessings, and even themselves.

Could it be that an additional benefit of adversity is to prompt us to heighten our sense of humor so as not to miss the lighter moments sometimes lost in our trials?

Have difficulties knocked you down recently? Be encouraged that your determination to get back up and face your challenge head on will make you a stronger person.

> One who gains strength by overcoming obstacles possesses the only strength which can overcome adversity.
>
> Albert Schweitzer[4]

Section Ten

RISKS: BREAK NEW GROUND

Chapter 37

IT'S NOT THAT BAD!

I knew a man who grabbed a cat by the tail and learned 40 percent more about cats than the man who didn't.

Mark Twain[1]

I CAN SPEAK WITH EXPERIENTIAL AUTHORITY on the subject of mistakes. Although I'm not an advocate for making dumb mistakes on purpose, I've undoubtedly learned what to do and what not to do by doing what didn't work. And, if you're making any moves toward your goals or attempting to do things you've never done before, mistakes have probably become a normal part of your inventory.

Motivational speaker Les Brown reminds us, "In order to get where you don't know you can go, you have to make mistakes to find out what you don't know."[2] I know mistakes can be embarrassing, painful and time consuming, but they are also marvelous teachers. In fact, going too long without a classic goof up might be a serious indication that you've stopped learning, squelched your curiosity, or have settled into a comfort zone. It means you're aiming far too low and passing up the opportunity to pursue new levels of performance. That's dangerous. In fact, any one of these factors is the most serious mistake of all.

Mistakes are learning tools, growing pains, and character builders you encounter on the way to your goals. They are friends most people would rather avoid. But friends help you find out how good you really are. As Nelson Boswell observed, "The difference between greatness and mediocrity is often how an individual views mistakes."[3]

To help you keep mistakes in perspective, Goldie Hawn says, "Once you can laugh at your own weaknesses, you can move forward. Comedy breaks down walls. It opens up people. If you're good, you can fill up those openings with something positive. Maybe you can combat some of the ugliness in the world."[4]

New Women magazine declared Linda Evans the winner of the "Most Embarrassing Moment Contest." Here was her submission: It was Christmas Eve, and I was on my feet all day working behind the cosmetics counter. I decided I should find a place to sit for a moment. I spied a tall plastic trash can and plopped down, resting my feet on a cardboard box. I allowed my body to ease into the can. About that time a few customers came to the register to check out, but I couldn't get out of the trash can. I was stuck; I couldn't believe it. The customers came around the counter to help me—some pulled my arms while others held the can. Then my manager came to the counter, wanting to know what was going on. He said he was going to call the fire department, who blasted in with sirens and lights. My hips had created a vacuum, so they had to cut me out of the trash can with a giant pair of scissors.[5]

I guess you could say she got "canned" without being fired. I'm sure Linda would be the first one to admit that her mistake got her derriere in a jam.

How would you like to be Janice? She spent nearly her whole vacation sunbathing on the roof of her hotel. She wore a two-piece bathing suit the first few days, but always removed her glasses to insure an even facial tan.

After several days she decided no one could see her way up there, so she slipped out of her suit to get a full body tan. She'd just gotten comfortable when she heard someone running up the outside stairs of the hotel. She was lying on her stomach, so she just pulled a towel over her bottom.

"Excuse me, miss," said the out of breath, sweating hotel manager. "The hotel doesn't mind your sunbathing on the roof, but we would appreciate your putting your suit back on."

"I'm sorry if I've violated some rule," Janice replied.

"It's not that," the manager calmly replied. "You're lying on the dining room skylight."[6]

OOPS!

The pastor of a small church prided himself on being sensitive to the needs of his parishioners. Moments before the Sunday morning service, he overheard a man complain about back pain. His wife quickly explained that Jack was recovering from surgery.

During the morning prayer, the pastor thought of Jack and prayed that he might recover from surgery and be "restored to full function." Chuckles scattered throughout the church.[7]

Jack's surgery was a vasectomy. Even good intentions can turn into innocent mistakes.

According to the *Houston Post*, Ben Wofford caught a bass worth $21,786 on April 11, 1992, at the Texas Bass Championship Tournament on Lake Conroe. His 7.64 pound fish was the fourth largest fish overall, but according to Rule 6, Ben's fish didn't qualify. Apparently the fish was fine, but Ben wasn't. Tournament Rule 6 clearly stated that all contestants must wear the official tournament hat they were issued at check-in. Ben had opted instead to wear his "lucky" cap and left the tournament headgear in his partner's truck.[8] Ben's small mistake caused him to be denied any prize money. Do you suppose Ben still owns that "lucky" cap?

Read this Valentine's Day ad closely:

ROSE SPECIAL
$9.99 One Dozen Roses Wrapped
Free Delivery to Hospitals and Funeral Homes[9]

The next time you're tempted to respond to your mistakes by organizing a self-pity party, reflect on the clumsy, ridiculous, and self-deprecating boo-boo's experienced by others. Your slip-ups and bumbling acts might not seem so bad. At any rate, Charles Handy suggests, "It's not the mistake that hurts us, it's the grace we employ owning up to it that counts."[10]

"Nobody makes mistakes on purpose," says Leo Burnett, founder of the advertising agency Leo Burnett, Inc. "When you do make a mistake, I urge that you shouldn't let it gnaw at you, but should get it out into the open quickly so it can be dealt with. And you'll sleep better, too."[11]

> Every great mistake has a halfway moment, a split second when it can be recalled and perhaps remedied.
>
> Pearl S. Buck[12]

Chapter 38

MOVE THROUGH YOUR FEARS

People are never more insecure than when they become
obsessed with their fears at the expense of their dreams.

Norman Cousins[1]

W E LIVE IN AN AGE of fear. Horace Fletcher said, "Fear
is an acid which is pumped into one's atmosphere. It
causes mental, moral, and spiritual asphyxiation, and
sometimes death; death to energy and all growth."[2] Fear imprisons
people. Fear keeps us from moving beyond where we are and from
achieving our potential.

"Fear, to a degree," says Zig Ziglar, "makes procrastinators and
cowards of us all."[3] We all tend to possess mannequins intended to
protect us from our fears. As Edmund Burke said, "No passion so
effectively robs the mind of all its powers of acting and reasoning as
fear."[4] Swiss psychiatrist Paul Tournier agreed: "All of us have reservoirs of our full potential, vast areas of great satisfaction, but the
road that leads to those reservoirs is guarded by the dragon of fear."[5]

This powerful life-stripping, adventure-robbing barrier is inside you. It's not the world, your circumstances, your job, your past or the people in the present. It's the fear in you.

The bad news is that fear sticks with us even when there is no real, concrete, or visible reason. The good news? Fear is learned and can be unlearned. "Most fear is routed in ignorance," says Brian Tracy. "The more knowledge or skill you have in any area, the less fear it holds."[6] It takes courage to overcome this fear-producing ignorance, but Dr. Karl A. Menninger reminded us that, "fears are educated into us and can, if we wish, be educated out."[7]

The first and most difficult step in overcoming fear is courageous action. Professional boxing manager Cus D'Amato suggested, "The hero and the coward both feel exactly the same fear, only the hero confronts his fear and converts it to power."[8] Everyone experiences fear one way or another. Only the victor makes an informed plunge forward.

The great composer Ludwig Van Beethoven lived much of his life fearing the possibility of deafness. How could anyone create a musical masterpiece without the benefit of hearing?

When that which he feared the most besieged him, Beethoven became frantic with anxiety. He consulted the specialists of his day and attempted every suggested remedy. Nothing worked.

Beethoven soon found himself living in a world of total quietness. He mustered the courage to move through his fear and the reality of deafness to write some of his finest musical masterpieces. The deafness shut out all distractions and the melodies flowed like never before. That which he had feared became a great asset.[9]

Many people discover, when coming face to face with their fear, that their *fear of fear* was the only real fear. Fear possesses the powerful ability to hold us back, keep our talents in check, and cause us to miss life's fruit.

I would, in no way, want to give you the impression that fear can be mastered once and for all. Each time an event arises that surfaces your fear, you'll have to battle self-talk, imagination, expectations, and the memory of past experiences. Mentally work through the worst that could happen and the best possible thing that could happen if you were successful. Be realistic, and if at all possible, move forward. Fear is not overcome by merely thinking positively. Action will reduce anxiety and tension, resulting in increased confidence and control.

"I believe that anyone can conquer fear," encouraged Eleanor Roosevelt, "by doing the things he fears to do, provided he keeps doing them until he gets a record of successful experiences behind him."[10]

Realize that fear causes you to seek a comfort zone that holds you back from all that life has in store for you. Action propels you past these limitations toward the attainment of your goals and dreams. Move through your fears toward the realization of what you want, and act as if it were impossible to fail.

> What success really means is looking failure in the face and tossing the dice anyway. You may be the only person who ever knows how the dice come up, but in that knowledge you have something that millions of people will never have—because they were afraid to try.
>
> Writer's Digest[11]

Chapter 39

SPRING BACK TO LIFE

Dreams have only one owner at a time. That's why dreamers are lonely.

Erma Bombeck[1]

MY BOSS, FRIEND, AND COMPANY owner Jack Vetter and I were sitting next to each other at a conference. We were listening to a keynote speaker who was entertaining and intent on challenging us to take our lives to the next level.

He blurted out a comment that simultaneously captured both of our attention. "80 percent of the population by age thirty-eight years old quits dreaming."

Jack immediately responded (loud enough for me to hear), "Oh no!"

"Oh no!" is right. How and why would we allow this to happen? Don't people believe the late Eleanor Roosevelt who said, "The future belongs to those who believe in the beauty of their dreams?"[2] Maybe this heartwarming story will give you a feel for what I mean.

Daniel E. Ruettiger grew up in Joliet, Illinois amid avid Notre Dame fans. He dreamed of one day playing football for the Fighting

Irish, but friends reminded him he was neither academically inclined nor athletically gifted enough to attend Notre Dame. He believed them and forfeited his dream for a job in a power plant and a two-year stint in the Navy.

The death of a friend jolted this young man into realizing that life is too short not to pursue your dreams. Daniel E. Ruettiger, better know today as *Rudy*, set his sights on achieving the desire of his heart.

At twenty-three years old he enrolled as a freshman at Holy Cross Junior College in South Bend, Indiana. Rudy worked hard academically and achieved a grade point average good enough to be accepted at Notre Dame. He was moving closer to his dream and even convinced Ara Parseghian, the brilliant football coach, to let him join the football program's scout team.

The realization of his dream was so close, yet so far. Finally, in Rudy's senior year, after teammates anonymously advocated for Rudy with Coach Dan Devine, Rudy was allowed to suit up for the season's final game. Notre Dame had undoubtedly secured a victory against Georgia Tech. The game clock was winding down as a student in the stands starting yelling, "We want Rudy!" Soon a choir of voices started chanting in unison, "We want Rudy! We want Rudy!" With twenty-seven seconds left to play, Rudy Ruettiger ran proudly on to the field and proceeded to make the last tackle of the ball game. The team hoisted him to their shoulders and carried him off in celebration.[3]

Rudy's heartwarming story was captured in a movie by the same name and captures the power of a heartfelt dream. Rudy observed, "If you really, really believe in your dream, you'll get there. But you have to have passion and total commitment to make it happen. When you have passion and commitment, you don't need a complex plan. Your plan is your life is your dream."[4]

People who live life to the fullest believe in their dreams. They speak life into their hopes by developing action plans that move them in the direction of their dreams. Like Rudy, successful people expect their dreams to be a preview of coming attractions in their life.

The philosopher Goethe said, "Whatever you can do or dream you can, begin it. Boldness has genius, power, and magic in it."[5] Think about it. What one great thing would you dare to dream if you knew you could not fail? If you were guaranteed success in any one area of your life, what would that dream consist of? Now, do you want it badly enough? Are you willing to boldly begin? Are you willing to pay the price?

There is a big difference between those who dream and those who make dreams come true. Walt Disney had confidence in his dream, even though he stood many times at the brink of financial ruin. He was emotionally committed to see it through, and his passion overcame the insurmountable obstacles he encountered.

Dreamers measure everything they do in their lives by whether or not it contributes to their dream. Dreamers become incredibly focused people. Dreams put life into perspective. Even the mundane, tedious tasks that fill our day become opportunities to pursue our dreams. Everything we do contributes to the fulfillment of those mental dreams and heartfelt wishes. Without a dream, we struggle to see beyond today. Life is a repetitive motion. Dreams wake you up, revive your spirit, and give life new meaning.

"I like thinking big," Donald Trump said. "I always have. To me, it's very simple: If you're going to be thinking anyway, you might as well think big."[6] It's a tragedy when people don't think beyond their comfort zone. When that happens, we feel deadness in our hearts and a drying of our spirits.

So you've dreamed many dreams, but nothing has happened. Your days are filled with hoping, wishing, wanting, and thinking, but the dreams fizzle. This may not be popular, but the dreams you have realized are the ones you passionately pursued. Your achievements are the result of a concentrated effort. Turn your dreams for the future into reality by continually investing yourself in the present possibilities.

> Everything starts with a dream.
>
> Warren Buffet[7]

Chapter 40

LIVE LIKE THERE'S NO TOMORROW

Let us so live that when we come to die even the undertaker
will be sorry.

Mark Twain[1]

I PREDICT THAT EVERYONE READING THIS is alive. However,
some are more alive than others.

Winston Churchill's funeral arrangements included specific
requests from the prime minister himself. He asked that the funeral
begin with the playing of "Taps," the traditional military signal
played at the end of the day or the end of life.

When the funeral service ended, those in attendance were
surprised to hear what Churchill had arranged for the conclusion.
Trumpets began to play the familiar strains of "Reveille," the star-
tling call that awakens the troops at the beginning of a new day.[2]

Could it be that Churchill was sending a message to those who
gathered to pay their last respects? Many of us could use a periodic
"Reveille," a wake-up call. Even though the blood is flowing and the
lungs are pumping, the playing of "Taps" might be appropriate.

Inspirational speaker Tony Campolo presented this challenge to an audience: "Most of us are tiptoeing through life so we can reach death safely. We should be praying, 'If I should wake before I die.' Life can get away from you. Don't be satisfied with just pumping blood."[3]

Our goal should be to live fully in the present, focusing on the demands and opportunities of today so we can make life better tomorrow. To create a quality future we must begin the commitment today. Not "Someday I'll." Not "When I get around to it." Not "When things get back to normal." Not "When I have more time." Not "Once the kids are grown." Now! And not a half-hearted effort but a full fledged effort.

Italian economist Vilfredo Pareto introduced the world to the 80/20 principle.[4] This widely accepted generalization indicates that 20 percent of our efforts produces 80 percent of our results. Expanded into other areas of life, this principle suggests that 20 percent of the people give 80 percent of the money, 20 percent of the people do 80 percent of the work, 20 percent of the people accumulate 80 percent of the wealth, and so on. It might even be said that 20 percent of the people read 80 percent of the books, but hopefully they read more than 80 percent of the pages.

What would it be like to live an 80/20 life? I'm convinced there are such people. They probably consistently enjoy life 80 percent of the time. Well, actually not real consistently, but normally 80 percent of the time.

They give family, career, and health their full energy, 80 percent of the time. When they want to make changes, they hope an 80 percent effort will suffice. When 80/20 persons are expected to take on additional responsibilities, she is shocked by the expectation and hope she can be 80 percent successful. They are already working at 80 percent capacity and feel like they are doing more than anyone else in the department.

I think you get the picture: 80/20 people probably still live okay but they are passing up innumerable opportunities to reap the full benefits of life. It doesn't take a rocket scientist to realize you can increase the results in all areas of your life if you pledge to no longer settle for 80 percent. Although others may be affected, you are really cheating yourself by not living 100 percent of each moment.

There will be hours, days, and months when you will be tempted to return to an 80/20 lifestyle. Each time, remind yourself how important it is to live each day as if there were no more days to live. Defy the 80/20 principle, the current status quo, and renew your commitment to be a 100 percent person.

You cannot go back and make a brand new start. But you can start now and make a brand new end.

Don't start playing "Taps" yet. In fact, sound the "Reveille" and start living with an excitement about each new moment.

> Look at a day when you are supremely satisfied at the end. It's not a day when you lounge around doing nothing. It's when you've had everything to do, and you've done it.
>
> Margaret Thatcher[5]

Section Eleven

COOPERATION: BE A TEAM PLAYER

Chapter 41

Become a Trust Builder

You can learn good manners to deal with people, but you can't learn to trust people. And you must trust to be comfortable with them.

Peter Drucker[1]

D O YOU TRUST THE PEOPLE you work with? Do they trust you? The answers to these two questions will reveal volumes about the quality of your work environment. J.W. Driscoll said, "Trust has been shown to be the most significant predictor of individuals' satisfaction with their organization."[2]

Trust between co-workers isn't just a nicety; trust is a mandatory ingredient for relationships to grow. "Without trust, there can be no cooperation between people, teams, departments, divisions," wrote quality expert Edwards Deming. "Without trust, each component will protect its own immediate interests to its own long-term detriment, and to the detriment of the entire system."[3] Consider that advice from a person who helped countless companies pursue their optimum performance. Deming's experience revealed the universal importance of trust to achieve quality, innovation, service, and productivity.

Low trust environments struggle with rampant turnover, absenteeism, unresolved conflict, low morale, dissatisfied customers, and a direct negative impact on the bottom line. In low trust environments, people tell you what you want to hear. There is apathy, backbiting, and disloyalty. Defensiveness, territorialism, and an unwillingness to take responsibility for mistakes are common place. People live in fear and suspicion. The ramifications are endless, inevitable, and costly.

Webster's defines trust as "assured reliance on the character, ability, strength, or trust of someone or something."[4] In other words, trust means to have faith in, or to believe in, someone or something. Distrust and skepticism are subtly replacing belief and talent. Many recent events discourage you from trusting.

"Trust is a calculated risk made with one's eyes open to the possibilities of failure," says Robert Levering, "but it is extended with the expectation of success."[5]

I've hired hundreds of people through the years and have subscribed to one cardinal rule: believe in and trust people until they prove themselves untrustworthy. In other words, trust begins with me; with my willingness to unconditionally trust other people. This goes against the common grain to wait for people to prove themselves before you trust them. Trust will breed trust. Mistrust breeds mistrust. The surest way to help people prove themselves trustworthy is to trust them.

You can help build an environment of trust with others. Incorporate the following seven principles in your daily activities.

1. Listen to people. Attempt to understand their feelings, perspectives, and experiences. Always keep sensitive and private information confidential. Seek out others' ideas. We trust people who make a sincere attempt to understand who we are and what we are about.

2. Be there for others. When we make time for people, recognize their effort, celebrate their accomplishments, and value their opinions, a trust bond develops. Look for the unique talents and abilities in those you work with and tell them what you see. Don't spend excessive time on your own agenda or focused on just your personal welfare.

3. Keep integrity intact. Demonstrate through your actions that people can unquestionably believe what you say, know you will keep your promises, and can be assure you will be open with them. In other words, walk the talk. Be sure your attitudes and actions are consistent with your words. This is probably the most powerful method for obtaining people's trust.

4. Refrain from gossip and feeding the grapevine. Untruths, exaggeration, and backbiting quickly suffocate trust. Get the facts. Deal with reality rather than hearsay. The truth isn't always easy to deal with but, healing the wounds caused by misinformation is always painful. Nurture a culture of straightforward, open, and honest communication.

5. Respect other people's values. Diversity is a fact of life. You can't ignore it. Although you may not agree or endorse someone's lifestyle, learn to respect their position. When you know and appreciate what others believe, a candid relationship can be achieved. Close minded people rarely build open relationships.

6. Care about people. This seems so simple, yet we tend to get so caught up in the busyness of doing and meeting demands that people's needs often take a back seat. The payoff for taking the time to really care about someone's personal welfare is significant. Help others achieve their goals and maintain their self-esteem. Thoughtfulness, respect, kindness, and a belief in people will breed success and trust.

7. Mend broken fences. Be willing to admit mistakes. Ask forgiveness. Restore peace where conflict has caused tension. Unhealed wounds will fester and infect relationships. Resist pointing an accusing finger when things go wrong. Take personal responsibility. Make amends.

Like all other relationship components, there is no magic formula for making trust suddenly appear. Trust isn't something we give attention to from nine to five; it requires a way of life that consistently displays those core principles for building trust. It takes an incredible commitment to develop the persistence, the patience, and the discipline to hold a relationship together for the long haul. Trust lies at the heart of this endeavor; consistency is the path that leads you there.

> The best proof of love is trust.
>
> Dr. Joyce Brothers[6]

Chapter 42

WE ARE THE TEAM

The most important measure of how good a game I played was
how much better I'd made my teammates play.

Bill Russell[1]

DYNAMIC TEAMS ARE COMPOSED OF people who possess a
genuine desire to make the team look good. When team
members fail to grasp this concept, it reflects on the image
of the entire team.

A three and a half hour lay-over at Chicago O'Hare on a sunny
and warm April Sunday afternoon is not on my top ten list of "Most
Desirable Things To Do!" Unboarding the plane, my mind raced
through ideas that would help me endure this boring necessity.
Being a people-watcher holds my attention for a short time, and
then I'm looking for other avenues to pass time.

Bookstores always draw my attention. And my money. I found one
near my departure gate and decided to invest some time browsing
the latest titles, reading a few pages, and "sampling" the merchandise. Convinced an hour had passed, I re-entered the corridor and

glanced at my watch. It stopped running. No wait, the second hand was moving. Only 12 minutes had elapsed. Now what?

The smell of freshly brewed gourmet coffee is a second temptation to which I often succumb. Ordering the biggest cup they offered and purchasing an equally tempting pastry, I decided to make my way to the seating area at the gate and wait out my lay-over.

As I entered the end of the terminal on B concourse, my eyes fell on a young man sitting in a wheelchair wearing a heavy coat, zipped up to his neck. His head was cocked back, eyes were tightly closed, and it was evident he was soundly sleeping.

"How sad," I thought to myself. "Here is a young man who could be making something of himself. Instead, he's homeless and comes to the airport to sleep off his nightly activities."

I continued reading, periodically glancing over at the limp body that hadn't moved since I sat down.

What could he be dreaming about? Where will he go when he finally awakens? What awaits him in his day-to-day surroundings?

"Hey, Jimmy!" a powerful voice blared behind me.

The young man woke, startled.

"You on break?"

"No," he responded groggily. "Can't you see I'm working?"

"Then I need you to push this lady to gate B-2. She has a plane to catch in 15 minutes."

"Ah, man," he responded as he slowly removed his heavy coat and threw it over the bench next to him.

To my surprise, he was dressed in the uniform of the airlines I was flying with. I had to smile. Here I was, judging and stereotyping without having the facts. The sad thing is, the facts were as bad as my misguided conclusions. What I had just witnessed had to be a fluke.

To say he was excited about performing his duties would be a drastic overstatement. His eyes were open, but his mind hadn't told his feet to start functioning. He shuffled behind the wheelchair, slowly pushing his elderly customer to her destination.

I stayed glued to my seat to observe how this situation would unfold. Would the lady in her wheelchair make her flight? Would Jimmy return to resume his nap? How would the airline employees respond?

Upon Jimmy's return to the area (which took place as slowly as he had exited), a few cohorts arrived to visit. "Gees, I hate it when the old bag wakes me up," he told his friends. "I was really enjoying myself. What time is it anyway?" When the conversation with his buddies ended, he put his coat back on, zipped it up, and resumed his sleeping position.

I couldn't believe my ears. This was no homeless, destitute, unwanted person. He was an airline employee bothered by the command to wake up and do his job. When I left the area an hour later, his mouth was hanging wide open as he periodically engaged in a gross sounding cough/snore. Not one employee questioned his status as they paraded by. He lived and worked (I use the term loosely) in his own world.

I again looked at my watch. 1:55 p.m. My flight was scheduled to leave at 1:45 p.m. "Will the flight to Fort Wayne be boarding soon?" I kindly asked the service representative.

"I'm sorry, sir, that flight just took off."

"You say what!" I gasped.

"Yes, sir, I made the announcements. Weren't you listening?"

(How could I tell her I was so busy watching one of her airline's inept employees that I lost track of time?)

"Please check to see if the plane is still on the ground," I pleaded.

A call to the lower gate indicated they had just closed the door. "Run" she said. They will let you on."

Two briefcases in hand, I took off briskly down the stairs out into the breezy afternoon and ran like crazy to my plane seventy-five yards away. Of course, one hundred eight pair of eyes peered in my direction as I boarded. I had not made any new friends by holding up our take-off.

The remainder of my flight was spent reflecting on how Jimmy's behavior clouded my perceptions of the entire airline. Not one of Jimmy's teammates said anything to him about his lethargic, unprofessional, lazy behavior. I wondered if they realized the impression he gave to the rest of the airline employees. Did they really want to be associated with such incompetence?

The more I thought, the more infuriated I became. But wait a minute. How many times are we guilty of excusing the performance of people on our teams with such justification as, "That's just the way Jimmy is." "Mary has always been negative." "Pete just isn't a team player." "Sally has never had much get up and go."

Coach John Wooden believed that if everyone does not accept his role and play it to the best of his ability, "the group as a whole is going to suffer." Through our consistent, active participation we can help our team develop a winning reputation.

> The main ingredient of stardom is the rest of the team.
>
> John Wooden[2]

Chapter 43

PRACTICE THE ART OF ENCOURAGEMENT

Flatter me, and I may not believe you. Criticize me, and I may not like you. Ignore me and I may not forgive you. Encourage me, and I will not forget you.

William Arthur Ward[1]

THINK FOR A MOMENT ABOUT your successful experience or an exciting event you had. Who did you want to tell? Think about a pressing problem you encountered recently, who did you go to for assistance? Think about the last time you were crushed by someone's unkind words. Who did you go to for support? Think about the most exciting thing that has happened in your life. Who was the first to know?

The names and faces of people who popped into your mind as you answered these questions are probably the picker-upper-people in your life. Picker-upper-people accept others for who they are, attempt to understand what is important to others, and provide the support necessary to encourage people to reach their personal goals. They do the little things that give us the courage to do greater things.

Basketball great Michael Jordan was asked by columnist Bob Greene why he wants his father to be in the stands during a basketball game. Jordan replied, "When he's there, I know I have at least one fan."[2] No matter how strong, self-confident, popular, or competent you are, feeling the support of a loyal fan can be just the encouragement you need to make it through a new challenge, difficult project or even a tedious task.

Likewise, you can be that loyal fan for others. People become so concerned about not being able to do great things for someone that they neglect to do the little things that can be equally as meaningful and effective. One of those "little things" you can do is to provide encouragement. Somebody once said, "Encouragement is the fuel for tomorrow." Encouragement rewards people for who they are and gives them hope in doing all they can do and becoming all they can be.

We all know how the smallest gesture, kind comment, genuine word of encouragement, quick compliment, or praise can make a lasting difference. And yet, we don't always take the time to let people know our heartfelt thoughts and give them a small gift of happiness.

Think about one person you work with who could benefit from a personal message that would make her feel good. Choose whatever quality, talent, action that you have observed in her life. What is it about her that you appreciate? Why are you glad to have the privilege of working with her? What has she done this week to make you smile, lift a load or add value to the team?

Make your message personal. Use her first name. Email her. Text her. Send a card including your words through snail mail. Write your message of encouragement in the first person and express how you feel about her. Be specific.

Help people believe in themselves. Build their confidence and self-esteem. Make a concentrated effort to see that people feel important and appreciated. Celebrate and get excited about other's success. Be a cheerleader. Point out strengths and contributions. Bring a ray of sunshine with you to work every day. Scatter it liberally wherever you go.

You can be a hero in your organization by becoming a picker-upper-person. Make it a way of life, rather than a one time event.

> We all need encouragement. We can live without it just as a young tree can live without fertilizer, but unless we receive that warm nurturing, we never reach our full potential, and like the tree left to itself, we seldom bear fruit.
>
> Florence Littauer[3]

Chapter 44

ACQUIRING AN AWESOME ATTITUDE

> The greatest discovery in our generation is that human beings, by changing the inner attitudes of their minds, can change the outer aspects of their lives.
>
> William James[1]

C ONSIDER THIS AN ATTITUDE CHECK-UP. Charles Swindoll hit the nail square on the head for me when he said, "The longer I live, the more I realize the impact of attitude on life. Attitude to me is more important than facts."[2] Tell me all the facts you want, but they blur who you really are. Facts can be manipulated. Show me your attitude, and the picture of you will be crystal clear.

Again, Swindoll: "I am convinced that life is 10 percent what happens to me and 90 percent how I react to it. And so it is with you...we are in charge of our attitudes."[3]

We have the privilege and responsibility to choose every day the attitude we will adopt for the day. That single choice dramatically influences the quality of everything we encounter. By activating our ability to control our reaction to life's situations, we will be amazed at how events begin to change.

So many people are one positive attitude away from having a great day, pursuing a dream, or rebuilding a relationship. People who have outstanding talent, impressive knowledge, and prime opportunities will undoubtedly experience average results unless they possess an expectant, "can-do" attitude. Attitude certainly isn't the only thing that determines success, but it is an important something.

For those people who need a few bullet points or specific strategies, here you go...

Expect the best. People who expect things to always go bad will not be disappointed. Positive expectations adjust your views on life and allow you the flexibility to enjoy the blessings and deal with challenges. W. Clement Stone, the multimillionaire, is famous for being an "inverse paranoid." This is someone who believes that the world is conspiring to do him good. How refreshing. Seeing every situation as being heaven-sent would certainly put a new face on life's experiences.

Years ago, I read about a man who lived on the outskirts of town. He developed quite a business selling hot dogs along the side of the road. The man was hard of hearing so never listened to the radio. He had trouble with his vision, so he never read a newspaper. But he knew how to sell hot dogs and had a booming business.

He built attractive signs and put them up along the highway advertising his delicious hot dogs. He stood along the side of the road and solicited every person who passed by to try his fabulous hot dogs. People bought his hot dogs and made frequent return visits. He increased his meat and bun orders, and he bought a bigger grill to prepare his famous dogs. The business was a resounding success. He made enough money to educate his son at one of the finest colleges.

Unfortunately, the son came home upon graduation as an educated pessimist (the worst kind). He observed his father's business and then remarked, "Father, haven't you been listening to the radio? Haven't you followed the stories in the newspaper? We're in the middle of a huge recession. Businesses are failing all around the country."

The father was astounded at his son's wisdom. He thought, "Well, my son's been to college. He reads the paper and business journals. He listens to the radio and keeps himself well informed. He must know what he is talking about." So the father cut back on his meat and bun order, removed his roadside signs, and no longer stood alongside the road to promote his hot dogs.

Of course, his sales fell dramatically. "You're right, son," the father said to his boy. "It's a good thing you came home. We are certainly in the middle of a huge recession."[4]

Expectation is often a self-fulfilling prophecy. Remember, the press has accurately predicated eight of our last two recessions. Sharpen your positive expectations. Expect the best.

Decide to be cheerful. I tend to respond to the request "How are you?" with "Wonderful" or "Fantastic." Periodically someone will say, "You can't always be fantastic." True. But I choose to believe I will be any minute. Choose to be joyful because every minute of life is a gift never to return. You only get one shot. It takes no more energy to decide to be cheerful than to decide to be downbeat.

Cheerfulness, and its negative counterpart, is normally visible on someone's face. When I was in the second grade, I had a fabulous teacher. Mrs. Krull was better to me than I deserved. I think it's because she lived across the alley from my grandparents. She was also a strong disciplinarian. One day during recess, Randy and I were pestering the girls. Mrs. Krull approached us and said, "Boys, when I was a child, I was told that if I made ugly faces, my face would freeze, and I would stay like that."

I was appalled at the potential outcome. However, Randy looked intently for a moment and then said to Mrs. Krull, "Well, teacher, you can't say no one warned you."

Looking downtrodden, depressed, negative, bitter, gloomy, discouraged, apathetic, resentful, and hopeless is pitiful. Smile! Be cheerful! By the time you're thirty, you wear the face you deserve.

Be a solution finder. Problem finders are all around. Rare are those people who can spot a solution in every problem rather than a problem in every solution. Like the old saying goes, "When you change the way in which you see things, the things you see will change." It's amazing how the slight shift in your perspective on things will alter habitual attitudes. Remember the words of Christian psychiatrist Frank Minirth, "The more you complain about the problems you have, the more problems you'll have to complain about."[5]

Talk positive. Listen carefully to your conversations. Your words, tone of voice, and non-verbals communicate your attitude to others and further ingrain your personality characteristics.

I read about a man who joined a monastery where, in addition to the vows of celibacy and poverty, he was required to take a vow of silence. The monastery was so strict he was only allowed to speak two words a year. The man lived his first year in absolute silence. At the end of the year, he was invited in to his superior for his annual performance review. His superior asked what two words he would like to share. "Food cold," the man replied. Then, he was back to his room and routine to spend his second year in silence. At the year's end, when he went in for his annual review, he was allowed to speak again. The two words he spoke were, "Bed hard." He then served his third year in silence. At the end of the year he told his superior in two words, "I quit!" and he got up to leave. His superior immediately responded, "Your decision doesn't surprise me at all. All you've done for the last three years is complain, complain, complain."

Talk Positive. No matter how few words you speak, make them positive. Quit complaining.

Develop a spirit of understanding and acceptance. Look around you. People who display a genuine, caring attitude and love for people normally display an affirmative, upbeat attitude.

John Maxwell tells the story of a mother and her adult daughter shopping one day, trying to make the most of a big sale weekend before Christmas. As they went from store to store in the mall, the mother complained about everything. Crowds. Poor quality of the merchandise. Prices. Sore feet. After the mother experienced a particularly difficult interaction with a clerk in one department store, she turned to her daughter and said, "I'm never going back to that store again. Did you see the dirty look she gave me?"

The daughter answered, "She didn't give it to you, Mom. You had it when you went in!"[6]

Ouch! Your attitude toward the people around you will determine the attitude they have toward you, which impacts the attitude you have toward life...you get the message.

Act as if. Act as if you have a great attitude. Act like the kind of day you want to have. Act like the person you want to become. A staff member once said to me, "I'm just waiting for someone to come along and motivate me." I immediately responded, "what if they don't show up?" Don't wait for a great attitude to tap you on the shoulder. If you want a quality, act as if you already have it and the chemistry to produce it will be activated.

Much of what we do every day comes from habitual behaviors. Our attitudes are no different. We have been perfecting our current attitudes over a period of time. If we desire to get different results out of life, then we will need to address current habits.

I came across a prayer recently that seems like an appropriate way to close this conversation. It said,

> *Dear Lord,*
>
> *So far today, I am doing all right. I have not gossiped, lost my temper, been greedy, grumpy, nasty, selfish, or self-indulgent. I have not whined, cursed, or eaten any chocolate.*
>
> *However, I am going to get out of bed in a few minutes, and I will need a lot more help after that. Amen.*[7]

One of the most important choices you make today is your attitude. You and you alone are in charge. This is the greatest day of your life. Do something positive with it—acquire an awesome attitude.

> You can't change from a negative mind-set to a positive mindset without changing from negative talking to positive talking. To do that you must change the input from negative to positive.
>
> Shad Helmstetter[8]

Section Twelve

JOYFULNESS: LOOSEN UP ... LIGHTEN UP ... HAVE FUN!

Chapter 45

AN ENTERTAINING
FLIGHT ATTENDANT

A fun working environment is much more productive than a routine environment. People who enjoy their work will come up with more ideas. The fun is contagious.

Roger Von Oech[1]

GOOD MORNING LADIES AND GENTLEMEN! Welcome aboard United Airlines flight 548, direct from Palm Springs to Chicago."

Wait a minute! My mind starts racing. I know it's early in the morning, 6:50 a.m. to be exact, but I was sure this flight went to Denver.

"Now that I got your attention," the voice continues, "my name is Annamarie and I'll be your first flight attendant today. Actually, we will be in route to Denver so if you were not planning to go there, now would be a good time to get off the plane."

"Safety is important to us so please take out the safety card in the pocket in front of you and acquaint yourself with the procedures. Come on everybody, take out those brochures and wave them in the air! (70 percent of the passenger chuckle and do as they are told. 20 percent aren't awake yet, and the other 10 percent are sourpusses). Thank you. Thank you."

"In the event that we mistakenly land in a body of water, a decision must be made. You can either pray and swim like crazy or use your seat as a flotation device."

"We will be serving breakfast in flight this morning. On the menu I have eggs Benedict and fruit crepes...not really, but they sound good to me. However, the flight attendants will be offering your choice of an omelet or cold cereal."

William Faulkner once lamented that: "The saddest thing in life is that the only thing we can do for eight hours a day, day after day, is work. We can't eat for eight hours a day, or drink for eight hours a day, or make love for eight hours a day. All that we can do for that long a period," he said, "is work, which is the reason man makes himself and everybody so miserable and unhappy."[2]

The attendant on flight 548 didn't possess Faulkner's attitude about work. She enjoyed what she did. Her entertaining approach to a normally routine, boring take-off procedure endeared the passengers to her. Think of the innumerable benefits people would experience were they to add this positive approach to their normal routine.

John Maxwell summed it up quite well: "I choose to have fun. Fun creates enjoyment. Enjoyment invites participation. Participation focuses attention. Attention expands awareness. Awareness promotes insight. Insight generates knowledge. Knowledge facilitates action. Action yields results."[3]

> I have always been able to gain my living without doing any work. I enjoyed the writing of books and magazine matter; it was merely billiards to me.
>
> Mark Twain[4]

Chapter 46

PUT YOUR WORK IN PERSPECTIVE

The master in the art of living makes little distinction between his work and his play, his labor and his leisure, his mind and his body, his information and his recreation, his life and his religion. He hardly knows which is which. He simply pursues his vision of excellence at whatever he does, leaving others to decide whether he is working or playing. To him, he's always doing both.

James Michener[1]

I'M ALMOST EMBARRASSED TO ADMIT it, but for many years I watched and enjoyed *Mighty Ducks*, the highly successful Disney movie about a youth hockey team that rises from anonymity to celebrity.

The movie opens with a flashback scene of a demanding, tough, overbearing hockey coach convincing a young player, Gordon Bombay, to attempt a crucial penalty shot. "If you miss this shot," he says, "you'll let me down and you'll let your team down!" The frightened boy manipulates the puck, takes his best shot, and barely misses the goal." The burden of that loss and the shame of letting his team down dramatically impacts Gordon Bombay for years to come.

Bombay unexpectedly becomes the coach of a group of struggling youth called the District Five Ducks. They know they are bad, and Bombay reinforces all the bad they believe about themselves. He berates them, insults them, teaches them to cheat, and continually pressures them to meet unrealistic expectations. He becomes the coach he had as a youth...and hates it.

Gordon Bombay gradually learns that having fun on the ice is a worthy goal of any player or coach. The *Mighty Ducks* learn to believe in themselves, support each other, refine their skills, and have fun playing hockey. Bombay works hard to nurture the enjoyment of the game in his young skaters, and in the closing chapter of the movie, he takes his team of Ducks into a championship play-off game. The opposing top-rated team is tough, big, mean, and coached by none other than his old coach, Jack Riley.

Riley's strategy hasn't changed a bit. He berates. He insults. He threatens. Bombay has endorsed a different approach. "More fun! More fun!" the team chants in the huddle with Bombay leading the cheer.

The Hawks and the Ducks skate to a 4–4 tie as the final gun sounds. But one of the Hawks has fouled a Duck player, giving the Ducks a penalty shot—one chance to win the championship.

Coach Bombay chooses Charlie Conway to take the final shot. Bombay's touching dialog with Charlie is the exact opposite of the conversation in the opening scene of the movie. "You may make it, you may not," Coach Bombay tells Charlie. "But that doesn't matter. What matters is that we're here. Look around. Who'd ever have thought we would make it this far? Take your best shot. I believe in you Charlie, win or lose."

Charlie grins, accepts the challenge, and sends the puck into the opponent's goal. The underdog Ducks win the championship.[2]

This movie portrays the type of environment and message needed in our organizations and personal careers. Willie Stargell, a retired baseball star, once remarked that at the start of a ballgame, you never hear an umpire yelling, "Work ball." Of course not. They always yell, "Play Ball!"[3]

I wonder what would happen if the people you work with, started every work day reminding themselves, "I get to go play today." Work should be a fun, marvelous, exciting game.

Instead, I run into people in a variety of careers who struggle with:

- Low self-esteem
- Feeling overwhelmed by job and people demands
- Uncertainty about their future
- Feelings of powerlessness to make things better
- Busyness without results
- A lack of meaning and satisfaction in their work
- Routine, monotony and boredom

People say they don't have time to have fun. They can't wait until the weekend so they can live again. Other people view their work as an interruption between free hours. Pressure, stress, and loss of control haunt many. Edward L. Bernays reminds us, "Never permit a dichotomy to rule your life, a dichotomy in which you hate what you do so you can have pleasure in your spare time. Look for a situation in which your work will give you as much happiness as your spare time."[4] What marvelous advice!

Mighty Ducks tends to put things in perspective. Work is meant to be enjoyed. In fact, when you learn to relax, enjoy the hours, refine your skills, give your best, and nurture those around you, a refreshing attitude of satisfaction will evolve. Try it. See for yourself that the pressure cooker many of us work in can be relieved by the soothing efforts of others, and by taking responsibility for self-induced negative feelings and thoughts about what we do for a living.

> Love what you're doing and don't retire....I would rather be a
> failure at something I love than a success at something I hate.
>
> George Burns[5]

Chapter 47

Refills Are Free

We can determine our optimum speed of living by trying various speeds and finding out which one is most agreeable.

Hans Selye[1]

T HE SHORT THIRTY-SIX MINUTE FLIGHT wasn't enough time for the flight attendants to serve beverages. Considering the early morning hour, most of us quickly made our way to the nearest airport coffee shop as soon as we exited the plane.

I took my place in line behind the other twenty caffeine deprived travelers. We were all entertained watching and listening to the server behind the counter. She was singing along with the oldies music on the radio, dancing, taking orders, working the cash register, flipping cups (before filling) and serving the coffee and goodies. If she didn't thoroughly enjoy her job, someone should nominate her for an Emmy Award winning performance.

As I approached the counter to place my order, she continued to entertain the customers with her perky personality. The man behind me jokingly commented, "You've got to get over this depression."

Misunderstanding his attempt at humor and unable to clearly hear what he said, she quickly replied, "Pressure? What pressure? I don't feel any pressure!"

I seemed to enjoy this morning's coffee a bit more than usual as I reflected on the events that had just taken place at the coffee bar. Here was a barista who had clearly decided her optimum speed of living. Because she was energetic, gregarious, fun-loving, and friendly at 7 a.m., some people were suspicious of her behavior. How could anyone move at that pace this early and enjoy what she was doing?

I'm finding it increasingly curious how moving slow, being sarcastic and negative, disliking your job, and dragging your way through life is considered normal. But show a little positive emotion, smile, and enjoy the day, and you're a candidate for being labeled unrealistic.

We each choose our optimum speed and nature of living. Unfortunately, some people have quit trying anything but the rut to which they are accustomed. That's their choice. It's unfortunate, but until they decide to put a little zip in their step, they'll continue reaping mediocre results.

I like being with people who like life. I enjoy the company of friends who enjoy work. I choose to spend time with people who choose to make the most of every moment they're breathing. Hang around these kinds of people and they will help you continually adjust and improve your speed of living.

I think I'll go back for a refill. I could use a little inspiration.

> If you are lucky enough to find a way of life you love, you have to find the courage to live it.
>
> John Irving[2]

Chapter 48

HAVE A LITTLE FUN

He who does not get fun and enjoyment out of every
day... needs to reorganize his life.

George Matthew Adams[1]

M Y WIFE GAVE ME A gift certificate on Valentine's Day for
a one-hour massage. I'd never indulged the services of a
massage therapist but it sounded like a fun experience.
So I called for an appointment.

Let me preface the remainder of this story with a bit of insight
about my personality. I enjoy a periodic practical joke that creates
a bit of humor or good clean fun. I normally reserve such antics for
people I know well, but this day a rare opportunity surfaced. I just
couldn't resist.

The therapist greeted me in her lobby and, after a bit of small talk,
she asked what type of massage I preferred. I weighed the options
and decided on deep muscle therapy. The therapist was cordial
and professional as she led me into the room and turned on some
"mood" music, assembled her lotions, and lit a few scented candles.
Then it happened.

"Glenn, I'm going to leave the room for a few minutes," she said. "Would you please disrobe down to your underwear."

I mustered a serious expression and replied, "I don't wear underwear!"

The laughter that followed, once she realized I was only kidding, probably stimulated more endorphins than the massage that followed.

I feel sorry for people whose lives are so regimented they are unable to produce, or enjoy, periodic doses of fun. I realize fun isn't for everyone. It's only for people who want to enjoy life and feel alive. For all others, there is tension, stress, ulcers, headaches, and boredom. The decision on which path to take sounds like a no-brainer to me.

Charlie Chaplin said, "If you've got something funny to do, you don't have to be funny to do it."[2] You don't have to change your personality to have fun. It does require you to look for the ridiculous, slightly humorous, absurd, entertaining events in everyday life. Having fun isn't something you necessarily learn; it is a perspective on life that you give yourself permission to enjoy.

As I drove through a small town in southern Iowa, I noticed a fun-loving radiator repair shop that posted this motto on their sign: "The best place in town to take a leak." I was equally impressed with some plumbers who approached their business with a bit of levity. Painted across the side of their van was this saying: "In our business, a flush beats a full house." That's the kind of plumber I want doing my work. And finally, a muffler shop in a small town in Nebraska made this attempt at fun: "No appointment necessary. We'll hear you coming." The people responsible for these signs have given themselves permission to express a perspective on life that produces a little fun.

Consider again the words of George Matthew Adams: "He who does not get fun and enjoyment out of every day—needs to reorganize his life." Is it time for you to do a little reorganizing?

A light heart lives long.

Shakespeare[3]

Endnotes

Introduction

1. Buck Rogers, source unknown.

Section One—Passion: Infuse Your Work With Passion

Chapter 1: Light Yourself on Fire

1. Stephen Covey, quoted on *Thinkexist.com*, http://thinkexist.com/quotation/motivation-is-a-fire-from-within-if-someone-else/362837.html.

2. *Joe Versus the Volcano*, written and directed by John Patrick Shanley, 102 minutes, Warner Bro. Pictures, 1990, DVD.

3. Paul Goodman, source unknown.

4. Reggie Leach, quoted on *The Quotations Page*, http://www.quotationspage.com/quote/1963.html.

Chapter 2: The Money is the Gravy

1. Bette Davis, quoted on *The Quotations Page*, http://www.quotationspage.com/quote/1772.html.

2. Denis Waitley, *Empires of the Mind: Lessons To Lead And Succeed In A Knowledge-Based World* (New York: Harper Paperbacks, 1996).

3. Charles Schwab, quoted on *Thinkexist.com*, http://thinkexist.com/quotation/the_man_who_does_not_work_for_the_love_of_work/10525.html.

4. Myer Waxler, *Good-bye Job, Hello Me* (Medina, OH: Scott, Foresman and Co., Publishing, 1987).

5. Robert Fulghum, *It Was On Fire When I Lay Down On It* (New York: Ivy Books, 1991).

6. Tom Brokaw, quoted on *QuotationsBook*, http://quotationsbook. com/quote/20891/.

7. Walt Disney, quoted on *C-Cubed: Career Consulting and Coaching*, http://www.ccubedcareer.com/index.php?page=what-is-coaching.

Chapter 3: Contentment Breeds Discontentment

1. William James, quoted by Brian Tracy in *Maximum Achievement: Strategies and Skills That Will Unlock Your Hidden Powers to Succeed* (New York: Simon & Schuster, 1995), 96.

2. Theron J. Hopkins, *The Eighty Yard Run: In Search of High School Football in America* (Twenty Town Press, 2004).

3. Quote found on milk bottles of *Wisconsin Dairy Industry*.

4. Charles M. Schulz, Peanuts, http://comics.com/peanuts.

5. Johann Wolfgang von Goethe, quoted on *thinkexist.com*, http://thinkexist.com/quotation/things_which_matter_most_must_never_be_at_the/180010.html.

6. *Pocahontas*, written by Carl Binder, et al, and directed by Mike Gabriel and Eric Goldberg, 81 minutes, Walt Disney Feature Animation, 1995, DVD.

7. Robert Kriegel, quoted on *Daily Celebrations*, http://www.dailycelebrations.com/habit.htm.

Chapter 4: There's No Need to Be Miserable

1. Lily Tomlin as Edith Ann, quoted on *Quotations*, http://www.theotherpages.org/quote/alpha-t3.html.

2. Norman Cousins, source unknown.

3. Rabbi Harold Kushner, *When All You've Ever Wanted Isn't Enough: The Search for a Life That Matters* (New York: Fireside, 2002).

4. Max Lucado, *He Still Moves Stones* (Nashville, TN: Thomas Nelson, 1993).

5. "Dean Martin Biography," *bio. TRUE STORY*, http://www.biography.com/search/article.do?id=9542166&part=1.

6. "How to Be Miserable," source unknown.

7. Greta Palmer, quoted by Paula Fellingham in "Happiness is a Choice," on *free article :: tutorial*, http://e-articles.info/e/a/title/Happiness-is-a-Choice/.

8. Dale Carnegie, quoted on *Thinkexist.com*, http://thinkexist.com/quotation/remember_happiness_doesn-t_depend_upon_who_you/10565.html.

9. Charlie Jones, quoted on WorldofQuotes.com, http://www.worldofquotes.com/author/Charlie-Jones/1/index.html.

10. Henry Miller, quoted on *Thinkexist.com*, http://thinkexist.com/quotation/it-s_good_to_be_just_plain_happy-it-s_a_little/340217.html.

11. Luci Swindoll, *You Bring the Confetti: God Brings the Joy* (Nashville, TN: Thomas Nelson, 2008).

Section Two—Learning: Good Enough Never Is

Chapter 5: Learners Will Inherit the Future

1. Ludwig van Beethoven, quoted on thinkexist.com, http://thinkexist.com/quotation/then_let_us_all_do_what_is_right-strive_with_all/192296.html.

2. Robert and Gerald Jay Goldberg, *Anchors: Brokaw, Jennings, Rather and the Evening News* (New York: Birch Lane Press, 1990).

3. John Kotter, quoted by Stratford Sherman in "LEADERS LEARN TO HEED THE VOICE WITHIN In the fast-moving New Economy, you need a new skill: reflection. Major companies—AT&T, PepsiCo, Aetna—are helping their people acquire it," *Fortune Magazine*, August 22, 1994, http://money.cnn.com/magazines/fortune/fortune_archive/1994/08/22/79648/index.htm.

4. Robert H. Rosen and Lisa Berger, *The Healthy Company* (New York: Tarcher, 1992).

5. Frank Lawrence, quoted by Jean Ashworth Bartle in *Lifeline for Children's Choir Directors* (Van Nuys, CA: Alfred Publishing, 1993), 203.

6. Eric Hoffer, quoted on *thinkexist.com*, http://thinkexist.com/quotation/in_a_time_of_drastic_change_it_is_the_learners/10724.html.

Chapter 6: Grow Beyond Where You Are

1. Tom Peters, quoted in "Continuous Learning and Workforce Development," *Developing Leaders*, Session 5, Issue 5, February 2007, http://www.tcdc-pa.com/upload/Session%205%20newsletter.pdf.

2. Ray Kroc, quoted by *BrainyQuote*, http://www.brainyquote.com/quotes/quotes/r/raykroc130750.html.

Chapter 7: Prepare for the Future

1. Dean Rusk, quoted by Dennis Lock in *The Gower Handbook of Management* (Surrey, UK: Gower Publishing Company), 182.

2. Jack Hayford, quoted by John C. Maxwell in *Success 101* (Nashville, TN: Thomas Nelson, 2008), 10.

3. Source unknown.

4. Peter Block, *The Empowered Manager: Positive Political Skills at Work* (Hoboken, NJ: Jossey-Bass, 1991).

5. André Gide, quoted on *The Quotations Page*, http://www.quotationspage.com/quote/1937.html.

6. Harvey Firestone Jr., source unknown.

Chapter 8: Settling for Nothing Less than WOW!

1. Walt Disney, quoted by Jack Kaser in "4 Hot Marketing Strategies that can Flood Your Business with Customers no Matter What Condition the Economy is In, " (Cincinnati, OH: NextLevel Business, Inc.).

2. Henry Ward Beecher, quoted on *Thinkexist.com*, http://thinkexist.com/quotation/hold_yourself_responsible_for_a_higher_standard/153224.html.

3. Charles Kendall Adams, quoted on *Thinkexist.com*, http://thinkexist.com/quotation/no_one_ever_attains_very_eminent_success_by/196961.html.

4. "Disneyland's History," *JustDisney.com*, http://www.justdisney.com/disneyland/history.html.

5. Russel H. Conwell, quoted on *QuotationsBook*, http://quotationsbook.com/author/1664/.

6. Oprah Winfrey, quoted on *The Quotations Page*, http://www.quotationspage.com/quote/1969.html.

SECTION THREE—OWNERSHIP: BECOME THE OWN IN OWNERSHIP

Chapter 9: Act Like an Owner

1. Rair Libeiro, *Success is no Accident* (Barcelona, Spain: Ediciones Urano, 2002).

2. Andy S. Grove, *Only the Paranoid Survive* (New York: Doubleday, 1996).

3. J.C. Penney, quoted on *Quotations for Last Names Starting with P*, http://www.tpub.com/Quotes/p.htm.

4. Brian Tracy, *Brian Tracy Articles*, http://www.briantracyarticles. com/principles-of-self-management/.

Chapter 10: Take the Time to Fix Your Leaky Boat

1. John Peer, quoted on *WorldofQuotes.com*, http://www. worldofquotes.com/author/John-Peer/1/index.html.

2. Short story, source unknown.

3. Harvey Mackay, source unknown.

4. Erik H. Erikson, *Identity: Youth and Crisis* (New York: W. W. Norton, 1968).

5. James Baldwin, quoted on *Basketballs Best*, http://www. basketballsbest.com/.

6. Al Neuharth, quoted on *QuotationsBook*, http://quotationsbook. com/quote/29818/.

7. Short story, source unknown.

8. John Maxwell, source unknown.

9. W. C. Fields, quoted on *Thinkexist.com*, http://thinkexist.com/ quotation/remember-a_dead_fish_can_float_downstream-but_it/298453. html.

10. John Foster Dulles, quoted on *Thinkexist.com*, http://thinkexist. com/quotation/the_measure_of_success_is_not_whether_you_ have_a/212109.html.

11. A. B. Simpson, quoted by Bruce Hurt on *preceptaustin.org*, http:// www.preceptaustin.org/philippians_illustrations_4.htm.

12. Lloyd Ogilvie, *If God Cares, Why Do I Still Have Problems?* (Nashville, TN: W. Publishing Group, 1985).

13. M. Scott Peck, *The Road Less Traveled* (Austin, TX: Touchstone, 2003), 16.

14. African Proverb, quoted on *The Dog Hause*, http://www.doghause. com/proverbs.asp.

Chapter 11: Don't Hold Back

1. Kenneth H. Blanchard, quoted on *goodreads*, http://www.goodreads. com/quotes/show/73713.

2. Mark Twain, quoted on *www.twainquotes.com*, http://www. twainquotes.com/Work.html.

3. Dwight D. Eisenhower, quoted by Donna Arnel in "When Employees do MoRE for Missouri, Everyone Wins," *MoRE*, http://www.training. oa.mo.gov/solutionsarchive/Solutions6sum03.pdf.

4. James Womack, quoted on *Thinkexist.com*, http://thinkexist.com/ quotation/commitment_unlocks_the_doors_of_imagination/211934. html.

Chapter 12: Making a Difference

1. Ruth Smeltzer, quoted on *Thinkexist.com*, http://thinkexist.com/ quotation/you_have_not_lived_a_perfect_day-even_though_you/223634. html.

2. Pearl Bailey, quoted on *AllGreatQuotes*, http://www.allgreatquotes. com/love_quotes260.shtml.

Section Four—Investment: Give Your Best to What Matters Most

Chapter 13: Take a Few Minutes to Think About Time

1. Patricia Cornwell, source unknown.

2. Bernard Berenson, quoted on *quotelady.com*, http://www.quotelady. com/authors/author-b.html.

3. Michael Fortino, quoted in "Consumer Economics Update: Fortino Study," *University of Missouri Extension*, http://extension.missouri.edu/ ceupdate/scripts/1996/12/dec-5.html.

4. Tor Dahl, quoted by John L. Eaton, "Managing Work vs. Adding Resources: An Answer to 'Why CEO's Fail,'" *R. Gaines Baty Associates*, http://www.rgba.com/article_2_why_ceos_fail.htm.

5. Johann Wolfgang von Goethe, quoted by Hans Finzel in *The Top Ten Mistakes Leaders Make* (Colorado Springs, CO: David C. Cook, 2007), 215.

6. Robert Eliot, quoted on *Winning Spirit*, http://winningspirit.com/ inspirational_quotes.shtml.

7. Peter F. Drucker, quoted by Kelly O'Donnell in *Missionary Care: Counting the Cost for World Evangelism* (Johnson City, TN: William Carey Library Publication, 1991), 225.

8. Albert R. Karr, quoted by John C. Maxwell and Connie Kittson in "Timely Advice about Time," *Leadership Essentials: Monthly Mentoring, September 2006*, http://www.growinguppink.com/notes/ September2006MMNotes.pdf.

9. Johann Wolfgang von Goethe, quoted on *BrainyQuote*, http://www.brainyquote.com/quotes/quotes/j/johannwolf150608.html.

10. Jack London, quoted on *The Quotations Page*, http://www.quotationspage.com/quote/5050.html.

Chapter 14: Learn to Schedule Your Priorities

1. Robert J. McKain, quoted on *Greeting Cards Resource*, http://www.greetingcardsresource.com/quotations-goals.html.

2. Johann Wolfgang von Goethe, quoted on *Famous Quotes and Famous Sayings*, http://quotations.home.worldnet.att.net/goethe.html.

Chapter 15: I Know You're Busy, But
What Are You Getting Done?

1. James J. Ling, quoted on *Bright Quotes*, http://brightquotes.com/goa_fr.html.

2. Henry Ford, source unknown.

3. Carl Hubbell, quoted by *The Simmons Firm, ALC*, http://www.rblaw.com/pages/quote.htm.

Chapter 16: Take Your Job and Love It!

1. Dale Carnegie, quoted on *BrainyQuote*, http://www.brainyquote.com/quotes/quotes/d/dalecarneg108921.html.

2. Warren Buffet, source unknown.

3. Leo F. Buscaglia, quoted on *BrainyQuote*, http://www.brainyquote.com/quotes/quotes/l/leobuscagl150305.html.

4. Ronald Reagan, quoted on *BrainyQuote*, http://www.brainyquote.com/quotes/keywords/hard.html.

5. B.C. Forbes, quoted on *SearchPro, Inc.*, http://www.searchpro.com/news_15.htm.

6. Andrew Carnegie, quoted on *Quotation Collection*, http://www.quotationcollection.com/author/Andrew_Carnegie/quotes.

7. Bob Biehl, source unknown.

8. Will Rogers, quoted on *Amy Ayoub & Associates*, http://www.ayoubassociates.com/.

9. Martin Luther King Jr., quoted on *Sermon Illustrations*, http://www.sermonillustrations.com/a-z/k/king_jr_martin_luther.htm.

10. Sister Mary Lauretta, quoted on *quotesmuseum*, http://www.quotesmuseum.com/quote/55960.

11. Calvin Coolidge, quoted in "National Affairs: The Price," *TIME*, March 18, 1929, http://www.time.com/time/magazine/article/0,9171,737526,00.html?iid=digg_share.

Section Five—Ability: Tap Into Your Talent
Chapter 17: Focus on What You Do Best

1. Thomas Wolfe, quoted on *Famous Quotes & Authors*, http://www.famousquotesandauthors.com/authors/thomas_wolfe_quotes.html.

2. Tide advertisement, source unknown.

3. "Joe Montana," *joe-montana.net*, http://joe-montana.net/biography.html.

4. Erica Jong, quoted on *BrainyQuote*, http://www.brainyquote.com/quotes/quotes/e/ericajong386949.html.

5. Charles Garfield, source unknown.

Chapter 18: Achievement Has No Finish Line

1. Dr. Charles Garfield, quoted by John C. Maxwell in "Leadership Wired," *Christianbook.com*, http://www.christianbook.com/html/leadership_wired/index0599.html.

2. John Wesley, *tlogical: Theology thru Technology*, http://www.tlogical.net/biojwesley.htm.

3. Thomas Edison, quoted on *goodreads*, http://www.goodreads.com/quotes/show_tag?name=edison.

4. Zig Ziglar, source unknown.

5. Dr. Joyce Brothers, quoted on *Power Quotes*, http://www.powerquotes.net/detail.asp?quoteid=927.

6. Will Rogers, quoted on *BrainyQuote*, http://www.brainyquote.com/quotes/quotes/w/willrogers103979.html.

Chapter 19: Dig a Little Deeper

1. Rear Admiral Richard E. Byrd, quoted in "Richard E. Byrd," *Wikiquote*, http://en.wikiquote.org/wiki/Richard_E._Byrd.

2. "Yates Pool," *Church of Christ, Smithville, Tennessee, Online Church Bulletin*, http://www.smithvillechurch.org/html/yates_pool.html.

3. Alfred Armand Montapert, *The Superior Philosophy of Man*, citation unknown.

4. Brian Tracy, "Capitalizing on Your Strengths," *Brian Tracy International: Achieve Your Personal and Business Goals Faster*, March 31, 2008, http://www.briantracy.com/articles/read-article.aspx?aid=85.

5. Og Mandino, quoted on *goodreads*, http://www.goodreads.com/quotes/show/10652.

6. "Abraham Maslow and the Biology of Human Values," *Holistic Educator*, http://www.holisticeducator.com/maslow.htm.

7. Johann Wolfgang von Goethe, quoted on BrainyQuote, http://www.brainyquote.com/quotes/quotes/j/johannwolf161315.html.

8. Friedrich W. Nietzsche, quoted on *BrainyQuote*, http://www.brainyquote.com/quotes/quotes/f/friedrichn159166.html.

Chapter 20: Rethink What You Think

1. George Matthew Adams, quoted on *BrainyQuote*, http://www.brainyquote.com/quotes/quotes/g/georgematt377543.html.

2. Robert Collier, source unknown.

3. Mark Twain, quoted on *Thinkexist.com*, http://en.thinkexist.com/quotation/life_does_not_consist_mainly-or_even_largely-of/295123.html.

4. Alfred North Whitehead, quoted on *GAIA Community*, http://www.gaia.com/quotes/1723/there_is_a_technique_a_knack/by_alfred_north_whitehead.

SECTION SIX—ATTITUDE: THE ANCHOR OF ATTITUDE

Chapter 21: Make Every Hour a Happy Hour

1. William Arthur Ward, quoted on *The Olson Group, E-News*, 1st Qtr., 2004, Vol. 1, Num. 1, http://www.theolsongroup.net/News/News1-2004.htm.

2. Lowell Peacock, quoted on *goodreads*, http://www.goodreads.com/quotes/show_tag?name=attitude.

3. John C. Maxwell, *The Winning Attitude: Your Key to Personal Success* (Nashville, TN: Thomas Nelson, 1993).

4. Norman Vincent Peale, quoted on *Thinkexist*, http://en.thinkexist.com/quotation/we_tend_to_get_what_we_expect/294417.html.

5. Dennis Waitley, quoted on *Leadership Now: Leading Thoughts*, http://www.leadershipnow.com/attitudequotes.html.

Chapter 22: Do What You Love and Success Will Follow

1. Henry Wadsworth Longfellow, quoted on *BrainyQuote*, http://www.brainyquote.com/quotes/quotes/h/henrywadsw121241.html.

2. Curtis Carlson, quoted on "Success—One Brick at a Time," *Positive-Personal-Growth.com*, http://www.positive-personal-growth.com/Success.html.

3. Michael Korda, quoted on "Success—A Journey or the Destination," *Articlesbase*, May 12, 2009, http://www.articlesbase.com/self-help-articles/success-a-journey-or-the-destination-913187.html.

4. Whit Hobbs, quoted by Cookie Tuminello in, "Get Geared up for Success in 2009," *Ezine @rticles*, http://ezinearticles.com/?Get-Geared-Up-For-Success-in-2009&id=1889557.

5. Barbara Stanwyck, quoted on *BrainyQuote*, http://www.brainyquote.com/quotes/quotes/b/barbarasta134574.html.

Chapter 23: Career-Building Principles

1. H. Jackson Brown Jr., *Life's Little Instruction Book: 511 Suggestions, Observations, and Reminders on How to Live a Happy and Rewarding Life* (Nashville, TN: Thomas Nelson, 1991).

2. St. Augustine, quoted in "Self-Improvement," on *Bright Quotes*, http://www.brightquotes.com/seli_fr.html.

3. Unknown author, quoted by Rick Warren in *The Purpose-Driven Church: Growth Without Compromising Your Message & Mission* (Grand Rapids, MI: Zondervan, 1995), 68.

4. Herb Cohen, *Herb Cohen: Negotiating and Selling*, http://www.herbcohenonline.com/index.htm.

5. Michael Jordan, quoted by Kent Shaffer in "From Good to Great According to Michael Jordan," *KentShaffer.com*, http://www.kentshaffer.com/from-good-to-great-according-to-michael-jordan/.

6. Billy Martin, source unknown.

7. Frank Lloyd Wright, quoted on *Thinkexist.com*, http://thinkexist.com/quotation/i_know_the_price_of_success-dedication-hard_work/168180.html.

8. Jimmy Johnson, source unknown.

9. Bruce Springsteen, quoted on "What is the best quote a rockstar ever said?" *Yahoo! Answers*, http://answers.yahoo.com/question/index?qid=20070510025917AAkDmPL.

10. Peace Corps Commercial, source unknown.

11. Alan Loy McGinnis, "Find Success in Your Life," *findsuccess.com*, http://www.find-success.com/.

12. Joanne C. Jones, source unknown.

13. St. Francis of Assisi, quoted on *BrainyQuote*, http://www. brainyquote.com/quotes/quotes/s/stfrancis109569.html.

14. Will Rogers, quoted on *BrainyQuote*, http://www.brainyquote.com/ quotes/quotes/w/willrogers121104.html.

15. Ken Blanchard and Don Shula, *Everyone's a Coach: Five Business Secrets for High-Performance Coaching* (New York: Harper Collins, 1996), 22.

16. Zig Ziglar, source unknown.

17. Mark Twain, quoted on *Bright Quotes*, http://www.brightquotes. com/tea_fr.html.

18. Michael Korda, quoted on *Brainy Quote*, http://www.brainyquote. com/quotes/quotes/m/michaelkor101731.html.

19. Bern Williams, quoted in "Have a Laugh on Us," Volume 2, http:// www.sleep-aid-tips.com/support-files/have-a-laugh-on-us-vol-2.pdf.

20. Ed Cole, quoted on "Life and Love and Why: A Reason to Start Over New," http://www.freewebs.com/krystallynn21/wisdomandsomepoems. htm.

21. Zig Ziglar, quoted on *The RealGoalGetter: Goal Setting Made Simple—How to Get What You Want*, http://realgoalgetter.com/ self-discipline-the-engine-of-personal-freedom.

22. Vince Lombardi, *The Official Website of Vince Lombardi*, http:// www.vincelombardi.com/about/quotes2.htm.

23. Corrie Ten Boom, quoted on *BrainyQuote*, http://www.brainyquote. com/quotes/quotes/c/corrietenb381186.html.

24. Christopher Chapmen, quoted by Jon Mundy in "Money and Jesus," *Institute for Personal Religion*, http://www.miraclesmagazine.org/ Articles/2009/Money%20and%20Jesus.htm.

25. Anne Morrow Lindbergh, quoted on *famouscreativewomen.com*, http://famouscreativewomen.com/one/157d.htm.

26. Jon Bon Jovi, source unknown.

27. Erma Bombeck, quoted on *goodreads*, http://www.goodreads.com/ author/quotes/11882.Erma_Bombeck.

Chapter 24: Know What You Value and Live It

1. Charlie "Tremendous" Jones, source unknown.

2. *The Queen Mary*, http://www.queenmary.com/index. php?page=1929.

3. Carl Rogers, quoted in "Who's Life is This Anyway?" *Utah State University*, http://www.usu.edu/arc/idea_sheets/whose_life.cfm.

4. Joe Batten, quoted on *QuotationsBook*, http://quotationsbook.com/ quote/35502/.

5. Jimmy Carter, quoted on *BrainyQuote*, http://www.brainyquote. com/quotes/quotes/j/jimmycarte121086.html.

6. Anthony Robbins, *Unlimited Power: the New Science of Personal Achievement* (New York: Simon & Schuster Audio, 2000).

SECTION SEVEN—IMPROVEMENT: BUILD A BETTER YOU

Chapter 25: Pay Attention to Who You Are

1. Bill Hybels, source unknown.

2. Robert A. Cook, quoted in "No Sweeter Name," *Ministry Elements*, http://ministryelements.com/index.php?option=com_content&task= view&id=16&Itemid=2.

3. John Morley, quoted on *BrainyQuote*, http://www.brainyquote.com/ quotes/quotes/j/johnmorley104286.html.

4. Bobby Richardson, source unknown.

5. Sam Ewing, quoted on *BrainyQuote*, http://www.brainyquote.com/ quotes/quotes/s/samewing104937.html.

Chapter 26: Getting a Better View of Yourself

1. Nancy Kerrigan, quoted on *The Quotations Page*, http://www. quotationspage.com/quote/3866.html.

2. Story, quoted by W. Herschel Ford in *Simple Sermons for Sunday Morning* (Ada, MI: Baker Books, 2001).

3. Joe Batten, source unknown.

4. Brian Tracy, source unknown.

5. Charles Spurgeon, *Charles Spurgeon Quotes*, http://www.theologue. org/quotes/SpurgeonQuotes.htm.

6. Ava Garder, quoted on "Like Father Like Son," *home.att.net*, http:// home.att.net/~churchactivities/LikeFatherLikeSon.htm.

7. Norman Vincent Peale, quoted on *QuotationsBook*, http://www. quotationsbook.com/quote/6816/.

8. Dennis Waitley, source unknown.

9. Story told by Roger Williams, source unknown.

10. Zig Ziglar, quoted on *Finest Quotes*, http://www.finestquotes.com/ author_quotes-author-Zig%20Ziglar-page-1.htm.

11. Tony Campolo, source unknown.

Chapter 27: Be the Best You Can Be

1. Thomas J. Watson, quoted on *QuotationsBook*, http:// quotationsbook.com/quote/13133/.

2. John C. Maxwell, *Developing the Leader Within You* (Nashville, TN: Thomas Nelson, 2005).

3. Pat Riley, quoted on *BrainyQuote*, http://www.brainyquote.com/ quotes/quotes/p/patriley147929.html.

4. Fred Mitchell, "Dodging Doubt Like Tacklers," *Chicago Tribune*, April 30, 1995.

5. Oliver Cromwell, quoted on *QuotationsBook*, http://www. quotationsbook.com/author/1773/.

6. Peter Drucker, quoted by John C. Maxwell in "Finding Your Own Strength Zone," *Crosswalk.com*, http://www.crosswalk.com/ pastors/11578309/print/.

7. Alfred North Whitehead, source unknown.

8. Swett Marden, quoted by Zale Tabakman in "Do It to a Finish," *Zale Tabakman*, http://www.zaletabakman.ca/library/classic-authors/ orison-swett-marden/pushing-to-the-front-by-orison-swett-marden/ chapter-22-do-it-to-a-finish/.

9. Lord Chesterfield, quoted on *BrainyQuote*, http://www.brainyquote. com/quotes/quotes/l/lordcheste122762.html.

10. Kathleen Norris, quoted on *WorldofQuotes.com*, http://www. worldofquotes.com/topic/Mediocrity/1/index.html.

Chapter 28: Jump In...You'll Get Used to It

1. Lou Erickson, quoted on *QuotationsBook*, http://www. quotationsbook.com/quote/23622/.

2. Russell Baker, quoted on *QuotationsBook*, http://quotationsbook. com/quote/23479/.

SECTION EIGHT—ACTION: MAKE THINGS HAPPEN
Chapter 29: Complete Uncompleted Tasks

1. William James, quoted on *BrainyQuote*, http://www.brainyquote.com/quotes/quotes/w/williamjam157180.html.

2. Henry David Thoreau, quoted on *FamousPoemsandPoets.com*, http://famouspoetsandpoems.com/poets/henry_david_thoreau/quotes.

3. Lyndon Johnson, source unknown.

Chapter 30: Half Finished

1. Anonymous, source unknown.

2. Charles F. Kettering, quoted on *BrainyQuote*, http://www.brainyquote.com/quotes/quotes/c/charlesket124372.html.

3. William James, source unknown.

4. Sir William Osler, quoted on *Daily Inspiring Quotes.com*, http://www.dailyinspiringquotes.com/goal.shtml.

5. Andrew Jackson, quoted on *Thinkexist.com*, http://thinkexist.com/quotation/take_time_to_deliberate-but_when_the_time_for/12703.html.

Chapter 31: Filling Holes or Planting Trees

1. Anita Roddick in "I am an Activist," on *AnitaRoddick.com*, http://www.anitaroddick.com/readmore.php?sid=154.

2. William Arthur Ward, quoted in "CBS 2 Partners with Foodbank for Second Annual Drive," *Food for Thought*, Spring 2008, Volume 21, Issue 1, http://www.idahofoodbank.org/Monthly%20Newsletter/2008_SPRING_Newsletter.pdf.

3. Conrad Hilton, quoted on *Thinkexist.com*, http://en.thinkexist.com/quotation/success_seems_to_be_connected_with_action/201932.html.

4. Theodore Roosevelt, quoted on *World Wide QC*, http://www.wwqci.com/.

5. A. Lou Vickery, quoted on *Thinkexist.com*, http://en.thinkexist.com/quotation/four_short_words_sum_up_what_has_lifted_most/323498.html.

Chapter 32: There Are Only So Many Tomorrows

1. Michael Landon, quoted on *The Quotations Page*, http://www.quotationspage.com/quote/40036.html.

2. Professor Keating, *Dead Poet's Society*, written by Tom Schulman and directed by Peter Weir, 128 minutes, Touchstone Pictures, 1989, DVD.

3. Professor Keating, *Dead Poet's Society*, written by Tom Schulman and directed by Peter Weir, 128 minutes, Touchstone Pictures, 1989, DVD.

4. *Groundhog Day*, written by Danny Rubin and Harold Ramis and directed by Harold Ramis, 101 minutes, Columbia Pictures, 1993, DVD.

5. Jim Valvano, quoted by Pastor Steven Muncherian in "The Essential of Christian Character," *Muncherian.com*, http://www.muncherian.com/s-ja2v14.html.

6. Joe Kapp, *Search of Kapp*, http://www.joekapp.com/elmercado/DanCasey/Links/Search_of_Kapp/search_of_kapp.html.

Section Nine—Development: Success Is Where You Find It

Chapter 33: Developing Your Picture of Success

1. Jennifer James, *Success is the Quality of Your Journey* (New York: The Newmarket Press, 1986).

2. John C. Maxwell, *The Success Journey: The Process of Living Your Dreams* (Nashville, TN: Thomas Nelson, 1997).

3. Donald Trump, quoted in "Real Meaning of Success," *The Zimbabwe Guardian*, January 29, 2008, http://www.talkzimbabwe.com/news/130/ARTICLE/1470/2008-01-29.html.

4. William Arthur Ward, quoted in "William Arthur Ward," *Wikiquote*, http://en.wikiquote.org/wiki/William_Arthur_Ward.

5. *1993 Pryor Report*, source unknown.

6. "Biography," *Janet Evans*, http://www.janetevans.com/index2.html.

7. Brian Tracy Quotes, http://briantracyquotes.wordpress.com/.

8. Isaac Stern, source unknown.

9. Brian Tracy, source unknown.

10. Henry Fonda, quoted in *Quotes of the Ages*, http://archana.com.np/BookofQuotes-archana.pdf.

Chapter 34: What Impression Would You Have Made?

1. W. Clement Stone, quoted on *quotesmuseum*, http://www.quotesmuseum.com/quote/82187.

2. William Jennings Bryant, quoted on *BrainyQuote*, http://www.brainyquote.com/quotes/quotes/w/williamjen204116.html.

3. Somerset Maugham, quoted on *Quoteland.com*, http://www.quoteland.com/search.asp?query=Success

Chapter 35: The Makings of Success

1. Ross Perot, source unknown.

2. Margaret Thatcher, quoted on *BrainyQuote*, http://www. brainyquote.com/quotes/quotes/m/margaretth153841.html.

3. Dr. Tom Morris, *True Success: A New Philosophy of Excellence* (New York: Berkley Trade, 1993).

4. James Rouche, quoted in "Quotations about Success," *World of Inspiration*, http://www.worldofinspiration.com/ quotations/?pg=2&c=Success.

5. Jonathan Winters, quoted on *BrainyQuote*, http://www.brainyquote. com/quotes/quotes/j/jonathanwi100484.html.

Chapter 36: Face Your Challenges Head On

1. Orison Swett Marden, quoted on *BrainyQuote*, http://www. brainyquote.com/quotes/quotes/o/orisonswet121864.html.

2. Mother Teresa, quoted on *Thinkexist.com*, http://en.thinkexist.com/ quotation/i_know_god_will_not_give_me_anything_i_can-t/9211.html.

3. Gary Richmond, *A View from the Zoo* (Nashville, TN: W. Publishing Group, 1987).

4. Albert Schweitzer, quoted on *BrainyQuote*, http://www.brainyquote. com/quotes/quotes/a/albertschw155978.html.

SECTION TEN—RISKS: BREAK NEW GROUND
Chapter 37: It's Not That Bad!

1. Mark Twain, quoted by Tony Cooke, *Tony Cooke Ministries*, http:// www.tonycooke.org/free_resources/messages/quotes/quote3.html.

2. Les Brown, source unknown.

3. Nelson Boswell, quoted on *QuotationsBook*, http://www. quotationsbook.com/quote/26686/.

4. Goldie Hawn, quoted on *The Quotations Page*, http://www. quotationspage.com/quotes/Goldie_Hawn.

5. Linda Evans, *New Women*, source unknown.

6. Funny story, source unknown.

7. Funny story, source unknown.

8. Story about Ben Wofford, *Houston Post*, citation unknown.

9. Rose advertisement, source unknown.

10. Charles Handy, source unknown.

11. Leo Burnett, source unknown.

12. Pearl S. Buck, quoted on *BrainyQuote*, http://www.brainyquote. com/quotes/authors/p/pearl_s_buck.html.

Chapter 38: Move Through Your Fears

1. Norman Cousins, quoted on *Thinkexist.com*, http://en.thinkexist. com/quotation/people_are_never_more_insecure_than_when_ they/217237.html.

2. Horace Fletcher, quoted in "Fear," *mansioningles.com*, http://www. mansioningles.com/recursos44.htm.

3. Zig Ziglar, source unknown.

4. Edmund Burke, quoted in "When Fear Strikes the Workplace," *BetterWorkplaceNow.com*, http://www.betterworkplacenow.com/fear. html.

5. Paul Tournier, quoted by Rick Warren in "What Your Fears do to You," *CBMC*, http://www.okc.cbmc.com/fax/files/200406a_fear.asp.

6. Brian Tracy, source unknown.

7. Karl A. Menninger, quoted on "Karl A. Menninger," *Creative Quotations*, http://www.creativequotations.com/one/1034a.htm.

8. Cus D'Amato, quoted by John C. Maxwell and Katie Walley, "Feel the Fear and Do it Anyway," *Leadership Essentials*, http://www. growinguppink.com/notes/May2006MMNotes_Answers.pdf.

9. Ludwig van Beethoven, *Ludwig van Beethoven's Biography*, http:// www.lvbeethoven.com/Bio/BiographyLudwig.html.

10. Eleanor Roosevelt, quoted on *BrainyQuote*, http://www. brainyquote.com/quotes/quotes/e/eleanorroo402491.html.

11. *Writer's Digest*, source unknown.

Chapter 39: Spring Back To Life

1. Erma Bombeck, quoted on *BrainyQuote*, http://www.brainyquote. com/quotes/quotes/e/ermabombec130033.html.

2. Eleanor Roosevelt, quoted on *Thinkexist.com*, http://en.thinkexist. com/quotation/the_future_belongs_to_those_who_believe_in_the/13262. html.

3. "Daniel E. Ruettiger," *Wikipedia*, http://en.wikipedia.org/wiki/ Daniel_Ruettiger.

4. Daniel E. Ruettiger, source unknown.

5. Johann Wolfgang von Goethe, quoted on *goodreads*, http://www. goodreads.com/quotes/show/929.

6. Donald Trump, quoted on *BrainyQuote*, http://www.brainyquote. com/quotes/authors/d/donald_trump.html.

7. Warren Buffet, source unknown.

Chapter 40: Live Like There's No Tomorrow

1. Mark Twain, quoted on *The Quotations Page*, http://www. quotationspage.com/quote/2328.html.

2. "Reveille," *Our Daily Bread: Daily Devotional*, http://www.rbc.org/ devotionals/our-daily-bread/1996/02/03/devotion.aspx.

3. Tony Campolo, quoted in "Life Art Quotes," *The Painter's Keys*, http://quote.robertgenn.com/getquotes.php?catid=174.

4. "Pareto Principle," *Wikipedia*, http://en.wikipedia.org/wiki/ Pareto_principle.

5. Margaret Thatcher, quoted on *Thinkexist.com*, http://en.thinkexist. com/quotation/look_at_a_day_when_you_are_supremely_satisfied_ at/14143.html.

Section Eleven—Cooperation: Be a Team Player
Chapter 41: Become a Trust Builder

1. Peter Drucker, source unknown.

2. J. W. Driscoll, "What Matters to Whom?" *Reputation Institute*, http://www.reputationinstitute.com/members/nyc06/Pirson_1.pdf.

3. Edwards Deming, quoted by Randy Pennington in "Pick a Problem— Find a Leader," *Randy Pennington*, http://www.penningtongroup.com/ newsletter/internal.aspx?tid=487&ArticleID=18912&iid=2414&sid=0.

4. "Trust," *Merriam Webster Online Dictionary*, http://www.merriam-webster.com/dictionary/trust.

5. Robert Levering, quoted by Jerry Graczyk in "A Calculated Risk," *Business Network International*, http://www.bninewyork.com/content/ pages/coachcorner.

6. Dr. Joyce Brothers, quoted on *Thinkexist.com*, http://en.thinkexist. com/quotation/the_best_proof_of_love_is_trust/203793.html.

Chapter 42: We Are the Team

1. Bill Russell, quoted in "A Few Secrets of Success," *Veredus: Advancing Business with People*, http://www.vereduscorp.com/articles_may3.asp.

2. John Wooden, quoted on *BrainyQuote*, http://www.brainyquote. com/quotes/quotes/j/johnwooden382296.html.

Chapter 43: Practice the Art of Encouragement

1. William Arthur Ward, quoted on *Wikiquote*, http://en.wikiquote.org/wiki/William_Arthur_Ward.

2. Michael Jordan, quoted by Tom Fitzpatrick in "Young Guns," *Phoenix New Times*, August 18, 1993, http://www.phoenixnewtimes.com/1993-08-18/news/young-guns/.

3. Florance Littauer, quoted on *History's Women: Inspirational Stories of Women Who Made a Difference*, Vol. 3, Issue 14, July 4, 2002, http://www.historyswomen.com/archives/07022002.htm.

Chapter 44: Acquiring an Awesome Attitude

1. William James, quoted on *The Quotations Page*, http://www.quotationspage.com/quotes/William_James/.

2. Charles R. Swindoll, quoted on *Thinkexist.com*, http://thinkexist.com/quotation/the_longer_i_live-the_more_i_realize_the_impact/296740.html.

3. Charles R. Swindoll, quoted on *Thinkexist.com*, http://thinkexist.com/quotation/the_longer_i_live-the_more_i_realize_the_impact/296740.html.

4. Short story, source unknown.

5. Frank Minirth, source unknown.

6. John C. Maxwell, short story, source unknown.

7. Prayer, source unknown.

8. Shad Helmstetter, source unknown.

SECTION TWELVE—JOYFULNESS: LOOSEN UP...LIGHTEN UP...HAVE FUN!

Chapter 45: An Entertaining Flight Attendant

1. Roger Von Oech, quoted by Joyce Weiss in "Bold Solutions to Boost the Bottom Line," http://marketplace.issi.net/2007/304.pdf.

2. William Faulkner, quoted on *Wikiquote*, http://en.wikiquote.org/wiki/William_Faulkner.

3. John C. Maxwell, source unknown.

4. Mark Twain, quoted on *twainquotes.com*, http://www.twainquotes.com/Twain.html.

Chapter 46: Put Your Work in Perspective

1. James A. Michener, quoted on *Thinkexist.com*, http://en.thinkexist.com/quotation/the_master_in_the_art_of_living_makes_little/295791.html.

2. *The Mighty Ducks*, written by Steven Brill and directed by Stephen Herek, 100 minutes, Avnet/Kerner Productions, 1992, DVD.

3. Willie Stargell, source unknown.

4. Edward L. Bernays, quoted on *QuotationsBook*, http://quotationsbook.com/quote/10871/.

5. George Burns, quoted in "George Burns," *Weblo.com Celebrities*, http://www.weblo.com/celebrity/available/George_Burns/571985/.

Chapter 47: Refills Are Free

1. Hans Selye, source unknown.

2. John Irving, quoted on *BrainyQuote*, http://www.brainyquote.com/quotes/quotes/j/johnirving121146.html.

Chapter 48: Have a Little Fun

1. George Matthew Adams, quoted on *Famous Quotes & Authors*, http://www.famousquotesandauthors.com/authors/george_matthew_adams_quotes.html.

2. Charlie Chaplin, quoted on *Therapeutic: Recreation Directory*, http://www.recreationtherapy.com/tx/txaug.htm.

3. Shakespeare, quoted on *Daily Celebrations*, http://www.dailycelebrations.com/heart.htm.

About the Author

Glenn Van Ekeren is the Executive Vice President for Vetter Health Services in Omaha, Nebraska, a company committed to providing "dignity in life" for the elderly. For the past thirty years, Glenn's primary profession has been helping people grow. His passion as a leader is to create a work environment where people feel good about themselves, their jobs, the people they work with, the people they serve, and their organization.

As a professional speaker, he is known for his inspiring, enthusiastic, and down-to-earth approach for maximizing people and organizational potential. Glenn has also traveled the country providing more than one thousand seminars and keynotes to nearly one hundred thousand people. Glenn's motto in life is "to live every moment of every day to the fullest." His seminars and books will make you laugh, think, feel great, look at life in a fresh way, and be inspired to stretch toward your potential. His messages capture people's attention, stir emotions, and provide practical strategies for personal and organizational growth.

Since 1988, Glenn has authored several books, including the original *Speaker's Sourcebook* and the best-selling *Speaker's Sourcebook II, 12 Simple Secrets of Happiness: Finding Joy in Everyday Relationships, 12 Simple Secrets of Happiness at Work: Finding Fulfillment, Reaping Rewards*, and *12 Simple Secrets of Happiness in a Topsy-Turvy World*. He is a featured author in several *Chicken*

Soup for the Soul books, as well as the editor of *Braude's Treasury of Wit & Humor for All Occasions* and *The Complete Speaker's & Toastmaster's Library*. Glenn has penned numerous articles for various professional publications.

CPSIA information can be obtained
at www.ICGtesting.com
Printed in the USA
FSHW011745170120
66065FS